IN VIEW OF

GOD'S

MERCIES

THE GIFT OF THE
GOSPEL IN ROMANS

COURTNEY DOCTOR

Lifeway Press®
Brentwood, Tennessee

Published by Lifeway Press®
© 2022 Courtney Doctor

Reprinted August 2022

ISBN: 978-1-0877-4748-4
Item: 005833030
Dewey decimal classification: 227.1
Subject heading: BIBLE. N.T. ROMANS / SALVATION / CHRISTIAN LIFE

To order additional copies of this resource, write Lifeway Resources Customer Service; 200 Powell Place, Suite 100; Brentwood, TN 37027; Fax order to 615.251.5933; call toll-free 800.458.2772; email order-entry@lifeway.com; or order online at lifeway.com.

Printed in the United States.

Lifeway Resources
200 Powell Place, Suite 100
Brentwood, TN 37027

**EDITORIAL TEAM,
LIFEWAY WOMEN
BIBLE STUDIES**

Becky Loyd
Director,
Lifeway Women

Tina Boesch
Manager

Chelsea Waack
Production Leader

Mike Wakefield
Content Editor

Erin Franklin
Production Editor

Chelsea Waack
Graphic Designer

Lauren Ervin
Cover Design

Table of Contents

About the Author

Courtney is an author and Bible teacher. She received an MDiv from Covenant Theological Seminary in 2013 and is the author of *From Garden to Glory: A Bible Study on the Bible's Story*, *Steadfast: A Devotional Bible Study on the Book of James*, and co-author of *Remember Your Joy: A Bible Study of Salvation Stories in the Old Testament*. She currently serves as the Coordinator of Women's Initiatives for The Gospel Coalition. Her greatest desire in all of this is to be able to faithfully study, apply, and teach the Word of God and help others to do the same.

God has blessed Courtney and her husband, Craig, with four wonderful children, two amazing daughters-in-law, five precious grandchildren, and a spunky Bernedoodle named Walter. Find her online at courtneydoctor.org.

Dedication

To Craig: you, like Paul, are a man completely captured and captivated by the mercies and goodness of God. Your passion for the beautiful gospel of grace that God has lavished on us is a joy to behold. Thank you for all the ways you love God and love me. I am eternally grateful for you.

A Word from Courtney

Welcome! I am so excited to study Romans with you. Many people might shy away from this book of the Bible thinking it's just an academic look at doctrine and theology. But while Romans contains both doctrine and theology—and certainly helps us understand the glories of God and His marvelous salvation—Paul was not, first and foremost, writing a systematic theology book. He was writing a personal letter to a church—a group of new Christians in the capital city of the Roman empire—to instruct, encourage, correct, and compel them to continue in the gospel.

Romans is a passionate letter written by a man completely captured by the beauty and majesty of God and His glorious salvation. Paul wanted his readers (then and now) to know how amazing and all-encompassing the gospel actually is—that it's powerful, planned, eternal, and free. Paul also wanted his readers to rejoice and rest in the glorious ramifications of this salvation for everyone who is in Christ: peace, life, freedom, adoption, love, hope, and all the other mercies we'll see.

Paul's hope was to exalt Jesus and point his readers to Him. He wanted us to understand the depths of the gospel of grace and to know the hope of a transformed life. Because, after God saves us, He invites us to join Him on His twofold mission—working in us, sanctifying and conforming us to the image of Jesus, and working through us, sending us out to others with the good news of salvation in Christ.

Oh, friend, I need to be reminded of each of these every day. I need to grow in my understanding of the gospel of grace, to rejoice and rest in the way the gospel informs the moments of my days, and to join God in His work of conforming me to Jesus as He sends me with the message of this glorious gospel to the ends of the earth. Join me in asking God to do that in each of us through this study!

How to Use This Study

We are going to approach our study of Romans with an inductive approach—a method that will be helpful no matter what book of the Bible you are studying. On most days of study, we will first observe the text by asking, *What does it say?* Then we will attempt to interpret the text by asking, *What does it mean?* In the last step we will seek to apply the text by asking, *What do I do?* This order helps us slow down and really examine the passage. Let me further explain.

What Does It Say/Observation: As we observe the text, we want to notice things like repeated words and specific details and to note any illustrations. We'll ask the basic *who, what, when, where,* and *how* questions. If you don't know the meaning of a word, look that word up and write down what you learn. Also, write down any questions you have as you read.

What Does It Mean/Interpretation: When we move to interpretation, we'll ask questions about meaning. We'll consider the intent of Paul, the author, and see the passage through the lens of the original audience—the believers in Rome who heard it first. At this point, we are not asking what this text means to me; we're asking what it would have meant to them.

What Do I Do/Application: The last step is to ask how this passage is meant to transform me. We want to consider what God has done and then ask how He wants us to respond in return. Our responses might include: repent, obey, believe, pursue holiness, wait, trust, be still, speak up, give, go, or worship. We'll let the interpretation of the text inform the application of the text.

Each session is broken into five increments of daily study per week. Plan on approximately twenty minutes of study each day (or an hour and a half each week). Each week will begin with prayer—a time for you to ask God to meet you as you study His living and active Word. I've provided a prayer to start your study each session, but I encourage you to journal your own prayers throughout the week. Share with God your gratitude, joy, repentance, sorrow, questions, and commitments.

I recommend you have a print Bible in front of you, rather than using an app on your phone or computer. The Bible passages found in this Bible study book are mostly from the English Standard Version, but feel free to use whatever translation you prefer.

Here are some other features of the study:

Digging Deeper

At the end of each day of study, you will have the opportunity to dig a little deeper into the text. I've listed three other Scripture passages for you to look up and see how they relate to the Romans passage we're studying for that day. We want to be students of the whole counsel of God's Word, and this section will help us do that!

Definitions

You might come across words and phrases you are unfamiliar with or want more clarity about their meaning. To provide this insight, I've included pull-out definitions throughout each session and a glossary of terms as an addendum on lifeway.com/mercies. Note: these definitions are based on my personal study and experience. We will use **THIS STYLE** to mark these terms throughout the study.

A Closer Look

We will just begin to scratch the surface of Romans in nine sessions. We could spend years together in this glorious book. So, our thirty-thousand foot overview will limit the amount and depth of what we can cover. However, there are some passages, phrases, or concepts I want to call special attention to for a deeper dive together. These designated callout sections are marked throughout the study as "A Closer Look."

Memory Work

A memory verse(s) is provided each session. Spend a few minutes each day memorizing it. The discipline of hiding God's Word in your heart will bear much fruit in your life and the lives of those around you. And a little memory verse "quiz" is provided at lifeway.com/mercies!

Video Teaching

You have access to video teaching that provides additional content to help you better understand and apply what you just studied in the previous session. You'll find detailed information for how to access the video teaching sessions that accompany this study on the card inserted in the back of your Bible study book.

Feel free to take notes on these video teaching sessions in the space provided on the Group Session pages. If you're doing this study with a group, you can use the questions and prompts provided on the Group Session pages to help you review the previous five days of study and discuss the video teaching together.

I'm truly looking forward to studying Romans with you. May God powerfully meet you in the study of His Word. My hope is that you will behold the mercies of God in new ways, be transformed more into the image of Jesus, and rejoice more in the gift of the gospel that is ours in Christ.

Much love,

Courtney

You'll find detailed information for how to access the video teaching sessions that accompany this study on the card inserted in the back of your Bible study book.

SESSION ONE

Introduction

Session One: MERCY SPEAKS

WATCH Session One video teaching.

1. Believe that God has called you to this study.

2. Do the personal study.
   - Read   • Think   • Pray   • Apply

3. Show up to your small group discussion.

4. Expect God to work.

DISCUSSION QUESTIONS

1   Courtney said, "We do not study God's Word merely to be informed; we study God's Word to be transformed." Why is that important to know as you study God's Word?

2   Share a recent experience of how God used His Word to bring about change in your life.

3   When it comes to God's Word, which do you find the most joy in: reading it, meditating on it, praying through it, or applying it? Which do you struggle with the most? Why?

4   What are some hindrances, distractions, or obstacles you might face in being able to complete the personal study each week? If you're a Bible study veteran, what tips would you offer in how to stay the course in our study?

5   Do you expect God to work in you through this study? What is one thing you are asking Him to do?

 To access the video teaching sessions, use the instructions in the back of your Bible study book.

SESSION TWO

Mercy Calls Us

ROMANS 1:1-17

Introduction

Here we go! As we embark on this journey together, remember that studying God's Word is both an extremely practical and a wonderfully supernatural activity. As you show up to this study in very ordinary ways—maybe still wearing your pajamas or sitting at a desk eating lunch or hoping the kids sleep for just thirty more minutes—God Himself is at work. His Word is living and active; it's acting on you as you study. Whether you have followed Jesus for a long time or are just trying to figure out who He is, the Holy Spirit is moving, opening your eyes and heart, enabling you to understand and apply the Word. And, as we'll see later in Romans, if you are in Christ, your mind is being renewed and you are being conformed more into the image of Christ. So pray, ask for insight and wisdom, do your homework, and know that God is at work in you as you study His Word.

In this first session of study, we're going to spend some time grounding ourselves in the historical context of the letter—who wrote it, to whom it was written, and why. Understanding context is an important step in any study. We can't know what God's Word says to us until we know what God was first saying to the original readers (we'll talk more about this on Day Two). This first session will be a little bit different than the others because for the first few days, we won't be asking, *What does it say? What does it mean?* and *What do I do?* Instead, we'll spend our time getting to know Paul and the church in Rome.

As we work our way through Paul's opening words, seeking to understand why they're important, we'll end the session looking at his grand thesis statement in Romans 1:16-17, your memory verses for the week. My hope is that we'll see anew the power and **MERCY** found in the gospel of Jesus Christ.

MERCY
God's compassion, patience, and loving-kindness that causes Him to withhold what we deserve (wrath and judgment) and by grace give what we don't deserve (salvation and life).

MEMORY VERSE

For I am not ashamed of the gospel, because it is the power of God for salvation to everyone who believes, first to the Jew, and also to the Greek. For in it the righteousness of God is revealed from faith to faith, just as it is written: The righteous will live by faith.

ROMANS 1:16-17, CSB

Prayer for the Week

Father, Your Word is life itself. Thank You for not

leaving us alone but for speaking to us through

it. Please give me a mind to understand, eyes to

see, ears to hear, and a heart that longs to obey.

I praise You for the gift of Your Son and the life

that is ours in Him. In His name I pray, **Amen.**

DAY 1

From Whom?

READ ROMANS 1:1-17.

In my house we have two different artists' replicas of Caravaggio's famous painting, *Conversion on the Way to Damascus.* I love this painting because it reminds me of both the power and mercy of God. In it, Paul is lying flat on his back after having been knocked off his horse by God Himself.

We don't know if Paul was actually riding a horse, but we do know he fell to the ground, blinded by a great light. This drastic encounter was, ultimately, God's great kindness to Paul.

Paul was radically changed from someone who hated and persecuted Christians into a man willing to give his whole life to the spread of the gospel. God's mercy, majesty, and great salvation completely captured Paul. Keep this in mind as we learn the backstory of the man who wrote the glorious letter we're studying.

Read Acts 7:54–8:3.

Who stood by (giving approval) for stoning Stephen to death?

What did Stephen pray for (v. 60)?

We first encounter Saul (his Jewish name)—also called Paul (his Roman name)—at the stoning of Stephen. Prior to the events depicted in the painting, Paul stood by and approved of the killing of Stephen, ravaged the early church, contributed to the first great persecution of Christians, and literally dragged men and women into dark, damp, and dangerous prisons—all because he hated the name of Jesus and everyone who followed Jesus.

Read Acts 9:1-19.

Why was Paul going to Damascus?

How did Jesus describe Paul's actions?

What did the Lord tell Ananias about Paul (vv. 15-16)?

When Paul talked about the "*power* of God for salvation to everyone who believes" (Rom. 1:16, emphasis mine), he spoke from experience. I love Caravaggio's painting so much because it portrays the power of God, knocking Paul off his horse—maybe literally, definitely figuratively—to save him.

How have you experienced God's power of salvation?

As you saw in Ananias' reaction, many of the early Christians were skeptical of Paul's conversion and slow to trust its legitimacy. If I had been there, I might have felt the same way. Sometimes it's hard to believe that certain people have been saved.

Read Acts 9:26. What did Paul try to do, and what response did he receive?

Are there specific people you think of as too far gone, too hopeless, for God to save? Write down anyone who comes to mind.

If the people on your list were saved, would you rejoice or be disappointed? Explain.

Are there any sins you consider too heinous for God to forgive? If so, take a minute to write them down.

Read Hebrews 7:25. What is Jesus able to do?

If there are people whom you think are too far gone to be saved, please take a moment and pray for them. And remember, nothing is impossible with God!

If there are sins (your own or the sins of others) that you think are too heinous for God to forgive, please take a moment and ask Him to remind you that "he is able to save to the uttermost those who draw near to God through him" (Heb. 7:25).

Before we turn our attention to the text of Romans, let's note the dates and locations surrounding the writing of this letter.

Observe the following on the map on the next page:
- AD 33: Jesus was crucified, raised from the dead, and ascended into heaven near Jerusalem.
- AD 33–34: Paul oversaw Stephen's death.
- AD 34: Paul met Jesus on the way from Jerusalem to Damascus.

After Paul's salvation encounter with Jesus, more than a decade passed before he began the first of his three missionary journeys around the Mediterranean Sea and Roman Empire. Those three journeys occupied his time for the next fifteen years. From various locations on these journeys, he wrote the majority of his thirteen letters we find in the New Testament. The letter to the Romans, even though it's the first of Paul's letters we encounter as we turn the pages of Scripture, was most likely the sixth letter he wrote.

- AD 57: Paul wrote Romans to the Christians in Rome from Corinth, a town just west of Athens, during his third missionary journey (AD 53–57).

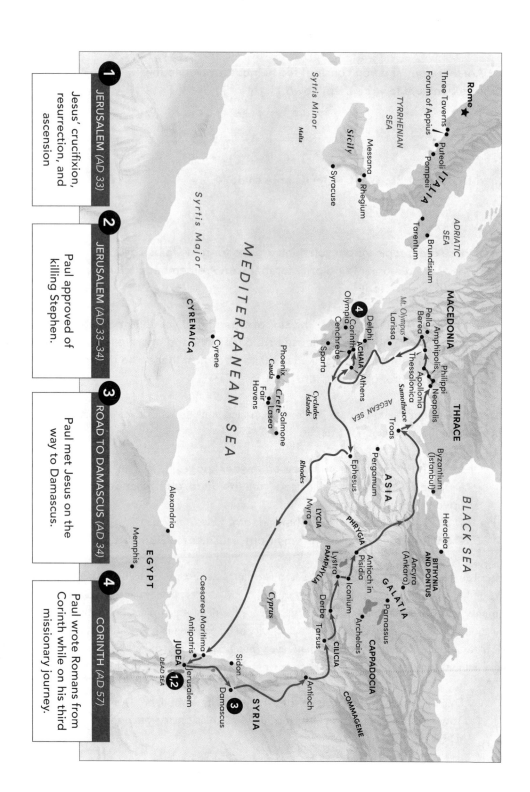

1 JERUSALEM (AD 33)

Jesus' crucifixion, resurrection, and ascension

2 JERUSALEM (AD 33–34)

Paul approved of killing Stephen.

3 ROAD TO DAMASCUS (AD 34)

Paul met Jesus on the way to Damascus.

4 CORINTH (AD 57)

Paul wrote Romans from Corinth while on his third missionary journey.

We are finally ready to open our Bibles to the book of Romans!

Read Romans 1:1. List the three things Paul said about himself as a way of introduction.

What do you think each description means?

None of us are first-century **APOSTLES**, but in what ways might each of these things be true of us also?

APOSTLE
The New Testament uses the word *apostle* to refer to the twelve men and Paul who "having seen the risen Christ, [were] a witness of His resurrection, and commissioned by Him, preach[ed] the gospel to all the nations."[1]

Paul, a zealous Jewish Pharisee, became a passionate follower of Jesus. His life shone with the joy of a man who knew he'd been forgiven, redeemed, and made new. As we read Acts and Paul's other New Testament letters, we learn that Paul, in his effort to proclaim this gospel that saved him, endured beatings, stoning, hunger, exposure, imprisonment, and was shipwrecked numerous times (2 Cor. 11:23-28). But, because he knew the power of the gospel, he knew those sufferings paled in comparison to the "surpassing worth of knowing Christ Jesus" (Phil. 3:8) and proclaiming Him to all the world. As you work on your memory verses today, may Paul's gratitude and passion for the gospel be yours as well.

DIGGING DEEPER
Check out these verses to help you better understand today's passage:
Acts 26:12-18 • Galatians 1:1 • 2 Peter 1:21

To Whom?

READ ROMANS 1:1-17.

One of my seminary professors said something in class one day that really rattled me. He said, "The Bible was written *for* you, but not *to* you." As you read that statement, you may react like I did—with indignation and frustration. I thought, *What do you mean it wasn't written to me?* I'd learned that the Bible was like a love note from God written directly to me.

Not only did I eventually come to agree with him, but his point proved tremendously helpful in my ability to understand, interpret, and apply the Bible in my own life. He meant that the words in the Bible, as we saw yesterday, were written by real people, to real people. If you were to read a letter I had written (back when that was something I did), knowing to whom I had written the letter would prove to be tremendously helpful. A letter I wrote to my mom would read very differently than a letter I wrote for a job application.

In the same way, if you read a letter I wrote to my husband when we were dating as if I had written it to you, you would be confused at best and uncomfortable at worst. But if you knew when and to whom I had written the letter, you would most likely find joy in the love expressed.

The people who first received the Scripture are called the original audience. We have to first understand what God, through the human author, was saying to them before we can know what God is saying to us. That was my professor's point.

Read Romans 1:7. How did Paul describe the people to whom he was writing?

Paul addressed his brothers and sisters in Rome with words that express our foundational identity in Christ. I like how Dr. Michael Kruger said it, "Our identity is built on three actions that God takes toward us in chronological order: (1) He loves us; (2) He calls us to himself, and (3) He makes us holy."[2] (The word used for *saints* can also be translated *holy ones*.)[3]

In what ways have you experienced each of these aspects?

- Loved by God

- Called by God

- Made (more and more) holy by God

Have you ever wondered how this church in Rome came to be? If Paul had never been to Rome, how did the church there get started? How had anyone in Rome even heard about Jesus and the events of His life, death, and resurrection—events that happened thousands of miles away in Jerusalem? There were no TVs, cell phones, Internet, planes, trains, or automobiles. So how was a church started? How did the good news about Jesus reach Rome so quickly?

Read Acts 2:1-12,37-41.

What day did this event take place?

Where were members of the crowd from?

What was the result of Peter's preaching (v. 41)?

Based on the events in Acts 2, describe how the church in Rome might have started.

Most likely, the church in Rome began with some Jewish men and women who were in Jerusalem on the day of Pentecost. They heard the gospel, realized Jesus was the fulfillment of all the Old Testament promises, and believed. They then took the gospel back home to Rome. As they faithfully lived out and proclaimed this good news, **GENTILES** living in the area heard and also believed. As the church grew, it comprised both Jewish and Gentile Christians. As we make our way through the letter, let's keep in mind that this was a multi-ethnic congregation.

GENTILES
In Greek the word literally means "the nations." It is used to describe anyone who is not Jewish.[4]

What were Jesus' last words as He ascended into heaven (Acts 1:8)?

What were the three geographical categories Jesus mentioned?

How was the church in Rome part of the fulfillment of Jesus' words?

Envision life during this time in Rome, the capital city of the entire Roman empire. Based on what you know of people (yourself or others) who live in large, influential cities, what characteristics might describe this group of believers?

According to Romans 1:7, what two things did Paul want God to give to the believers in Rome? Write down a definition for each of them.

Before you work on your memory verses today, reflect on God's plan to build His church and the ways He has done so through the ages. The gospel cascades down through faithful people, like those in Rome, who, by the mercy of God, heard the good news of Jesus Christ, believed, and shared this good news with others. You and I stand downstream from them, the grateful recipients of God's plan and their faithfulness. And, if we're faithful to proclaim the gospel, others will receive it from us. What a gift, what a privilege!

DIGGING DEEPER
Check out these verses to help you better understand today's passage:
Psalm 102:18 • Jeremiah 29:7 • Revelation 7:9–10

Grace to You

READ ROMANS 1:1-7.

Thanks to Twitter®, Instagram® stories, and texting, we're growing more and more accustomed to brief blurbs and snappy phrases. The short, pithy sentence captivates us. If we're not careful, we can "like," "heart," or retweet based more on the entertainment value of the sentence than on the validity of its contents. Conversely, the first seven verses of Romans are one long sentence! (I guess Paul's middle school English teacher forgot to teach him about run-on sentences.) Because we're not used to reading such a long string of ideas, we will need to slow down and pay attention in order to understand what Paul was saying.

What Does It Say?

We've already seen that Paul described himself as "set apart for the gospel" (v. 1). He wanted to make sure his readers began to understand what the gospel is—one of the main themes in his letter to the Romans. As we study together, we will learn more and more about both what the gospel is and what the gospel accomplishes.

When was the gospel promised?	
Where was it promised?	
To whom does the gospel concern?	
What is the result of the gospel through Christ?	
Where is the gospel to go?	

The gospel is all about Jesus, who He is and what He has done. But Paul wanted his readers to understand that while the events central to the gospel—Jesus' incarnation, death, and resurrection—were unique, the gospel is not new news. The Old Testament points to the coming of Jesus, and the New Testament proclaims that all the Old Testament promises have been fulfilled in Jesus (Matt. 26:56; Luke 24:27; 2 Cor. 1:20). This means that you and I, from where we stand in the story of redemption—after the resurrection and before Jesus comes again—have the key to understanding the Old Testament. The key is Jesus!

What Does It Mean?

How would you summarize Paul's description of the gospel in Romans 1:1-7?

How would you describe the relationship between obedience and faith? Why do you think he might have included this phrase "obedience of faith" (or "obedience that comes from faith" in the NIV translation) in his description of the gospel (v. 5)?

The relationship between obedience and faith is an important one. Faith comes first. We don't receive salvation through obedience, we receive it only through faith. God first gives us the faith we need to believe, and then He calls us to respond to this great gift by living a life of joyful obedience. Obedience flows from faith.

What Do I Do?

God's eyes have always been set on the whole world. He told Adam and Eve to "Be fruitful and increase in number; fill the earth . . ." (Gen. 1:28, NIV). He told Abraham that he would bless him so "all the families of the earth [would] be blessed" through him (Gen. 12:3). Jesus told His disciples to "go and make disciples of all nations" (Matt. 28:19, NIV) and be His "witnesses . . . to the end of the earth" (Acts 1:8). The plan of God has always been to make a people for Himself and for that one people to be from every tribe, tongue, and nation. Or as the disciple John wrote, "For God so loved *the world*, that he gave his only Son, that whoever believes in him should not perish but have eternal life" (John 3:16, emphasis mine).

In line with the heart of God, Paul longed to see the gospel go to all the nations. Paul hoped the Roman Christians would help send him to Spain to preach the good news there (Rom. 15:22-24). One reason he was so "eager to preach the gospel" to the Christians in Rome was because he wanted them to be eager to proclaim it with him to the ends of the earth (Rom. 1:15).

> In what ways do you participate in the spread of the gospel to the ends of the earth? Remember, this could mean sharing the gospel in your family, your neighborhood, your city, your country, or anywhere in the world.

Let's close by going back to that phrase "obedience of faith" in verse 5. One author said it "means bowing the knee in trusting submission to Jesus the Lord, both at the start and all through the Christian life."[5]

> If you are a Christian, describe how you are currently "bowing the knee in trusting submission to Jesus?" If you are not yet a Christian, what might be keeping you from "bowing the knee in trusting submission to Jesus"?

> Spend a few minutes writing down your understanding of the gospel, both what it is and what it does. (Don't worry if this feels hard. Romans is going to teach us exactly what the gospel is, so just take your best shot at it for now. We'll come back and do this again at the end of the study to see how your understanding has changed.)

If you are a follower of Jesus, you and I are to be ready at all times to explain to others the reason "for the hope that is in you" (1 Pet. 3:15). As you work on your memory verses today, think about what truths they teach us about the gospel message.

DIGGING DEEPER
Check out these verses to help you better understand today's passage:
Matthew 28:19 • Luke 1:68-75 • Luke 24:27

DAY 4

Thankful for You

READ ROMANS 1:8-15.

What would it feel like to receive a personal letter from someone famous, someone you admire but have never actually met? And what if that person began the letter by telling you how he or she is thankful for you, thinks about you (not in a creepy way, but in a kind, thoughtful way), prays for you, and is eagerly planning to visit you? How would you feel? I imagine the believers in Rome felt similarly.

Paul had never been to Rome, but we can assume the people in the Roman church were well aware of who he was. He was an apostle. He had been set apart to proclaim the gospel and establish the church. God also inspired him to write at least thirteen of the letters in the New Testament. When they received this letter, imagine the joy they must have felt to realize he sincerely loved them, knew about them, prayed for them, and asked God to allow him to visit them.

What Does It Say?

Based on verses 8–15, write down four to five things describing how Paul felt about the Roman believers.

I spoke with a friend recently who told me she wanted to intentionally cultivate more gratitude in her heart. To do so, she was paying attention to the joys in life and making a daily list of things to be thankful for. That's a great discipline to develop. As I read today's text, I realize that what we're thankful for and why we're thankful reveal a lot about our gospel priorities.

Write down specifically	
What Paul was thankful for	
What he prayed for	
What he longed for	
What he was eager for	

According to verses 11-12, what two results was Paul hoping his visit to the Romans would bring?

RESOURCE RECOMMENDATION
I'm Praying for You
by Nancy Guthrie

Paul didn't see his potential trip to Rome as a one-way blessing. He knew that he, too, would be blessed. Paul demonstrated humility in his expectations to both give and receive, teach and learn, encourage and be encouraged, strengthen and be strengthened. We need to follow Paul's example and adopt his humility in all of life, but especially in ministry.

Do you disciple or mentor others? If so, do you look for the blessing and encouragement in that relationship to be mutual, or do you see yourself as the solitary dispenser of the blessings?

Do you teach or lead? If so, do you, like Paul, expect to receive blessing and encouragement even as you give those to others? The Christian life is one of mutual interdependence on one another, and we do well to walk in the humility it takes to both give and receive.

What Does It Mean?

Why do you think Paul felt he was "under obligation" to others to preach the gospel (v. 14)? In what ways does this change the way you think about sharing the gospel?

Few of us like to feel obligated. We don't want to owe anyone or feel indebted in any way. But have you ever heard someone say that sharing the gospel is "just one beggar telling another beggar where to find bread"?[6] It's true. Think about that analogy for a minute. If you really were starving and you really had found a never-ending source of bread, would you—should you—have an obligation to tell other starving people about the bread? Yes! We all should feel that kind of obligation to share the gospel. As a carrier of the gospel, Paul had the life-saving news that spiritually dead, lost people needed to hear. So do we.

Paul said he was "eager to preach the gospel to you also who are in Rome" (v. 15). Paul was writing to people who were already followers of Jesus—Christians. Why do Christians need the gospel preached to them (us)?

One reason we need to hear the gospel time and time again is because we are forgetful people. We need to be reminded of God's love and grace every day. We need to be told over and over how to run to Him, rest in Him, obey Him, and love Him. I encourage you to faithfully attend a church that proclaims the gospel. Surround yourself with friends who remind you of gospel truths. Preach the gospel to your own soul. And run to God's Word every day to hear the glorious truths of the gospel message again and again.

What Do I Do?

Look back at Paul's words in verses 8-15. Perhaps there is a group of believers you feel similar toward. If so:

Why are you thankful for the relationship you have with them?

What is your prayer for these believers?

When you consider your relationship with them, what do you long for?

What are you eager to do for them to help them grow in Christ?

List four to six ways you think the believers in Rome and Paul might have "mutually encouraged" each other (v. 12). How do you both encourage and receive encouragement from others in the faith?

Think for a moment about the early Christians in Rome. Spend some time in prayer thanking God for their salvation. Ask Him to cultivate an even greater love in your heart for all of your brothers and sisters in the faith.

And don't forget to work on your memory verses!

DIGGING DEEPER
Check out these verses to help you better understand today's passage:
1 Thessalonians 5:11 • Hebrews 10:24-25 • Jude 20-21

I Am Not Ashamed

READ ROMANS 1:16-17.

Today we are going to study the two verses you've (hopefully) been memorizing this week. These grand verses have greatly influenced the likes of Augustine, Martin Luther, and many others through the ages. My hope is that as we study, memorize, think about, and discuss these two verses, our grasp of the greatness of the gospel will grow and our worship of the One who saved us will increase.

What Does It Say?

How did Paul describe the gospel?

The word for *Greek* or *Gentile* in verse 16 includes all the nations that are not Jewish. Knowing this, who is the gospel for?

What does the gospel reveal?

Briefly write what you learn about each of these keywords just from these two verses.	
GOSPEL	
SALVATION	
RIGHTEOUSNESS	
FAITH	

As you read these verses, did you wonder why Paul wrote, "first to the Jew, then to the Gentile" (v. 16, NIV)? Was he prioritizing the Jewish Christians over the Gentile Christians? No. Paul was simply referring to the chronological history of salvation.

God chose to work out His plan of redemption through the course of time, and He did it through the nation of Israel. We'll be reminded in the sessions to come that it was Israel who received the promises of God. The Jewish people were the ones with whom God entered into covenant. The prophets and priests were Jewish. And Jesus came as a Jewish man to the Jewish people first. That is what Paul was referring to—salvation came first to the Jew and then to everyone else.

What Does It Mean?

Based on these verses, how would you describe the relationship between the gospel and righteousness?

What do you think Paul meant when he said "shall live" (or "will live") (v. 17)?

Paul wanted his readers to understand that salvation can never be "earned." Nothing can be brought to God in exchange for salvation—no good works, no amount of money, no family legacy. Nothing. Salvation is always and only given as a gift to those who come empty-handed and believe God. We are saved by faith alone. And we continue to live in the reality of our salvation by faith. That was Paul's point: "the righteous" (those who have been saved by faith) are to (also) "live by faith" (v. 17).

What Do I Do?

I've been ashamed of the gospel before. The time most vividly seared in my mind was at a meat counter in a grocery store. Based on his conversation with the two people in front of me in line, the older man behind the counter was obviously sad about something. As I waited my turn, I felt the clear nudge of the Holy Spirit to offer him some hope from the good news of the gospel. But by the time it was my turn to ask for my two pounds of shaved ham, I had convinced myself to remain silent with several excuses. First, there

RIGHTEOUS
The state of being morally perfect and without sin.

GOSPEL
The good news that we can be made right with God through faith in the saving work of Jesus.

SALVATION
The death and resurrection of Jesus in the past means that we can be right with God in the present, and dwell with Him in the eternal future.

RIGHTEOUSNESS
An attribute of God. He is utterly perfect in who He is and in everything He does. It is also a free gift God graciously gives to all who trust in Jesus.

FAITH
The gift of God enabling a person to believe in Jesus and receive the salvation He accomplished.

were quite a few people in line behind me, and I didn't want to hold them up. Second, I wasn't sure where to start. Third, I didn't want to overstep into his personal problems. So I asked for my ham and walked away.

As I sat in my car in the parking lot, tears began to stream down my cheeks. I realized my "excuses" weren't the real reasons I chickened out. I was ashamed of the gospel. I didn't want the people behind me to think I was weird. I didn't want future encounters with the man behind the counter to be awkward. Basically, I cared more about what people thought of me than I cared about them. I'm ashamed that I was ashamed.

I find it encouraging to think that Paul had possibly, at some point, been ashamed of the gospel, too—and had learned not to be! If you, like me, have ever been ashamed of the gospel, confess it to God and ask Him to change you into someone who can say, with Paul, "I am not ashamed of the gospel, for it is the power of God for salvation" (v. 16).

What have we seen in Romans so far that can help you not be ashamed of the gospel?

In verse 17, Paul talked about something that we are going to learn a lot more about—the righteousness of God. Righteousness is not a wildly popular topic of discussion. If you're a Christian, you might even shy away from using that word when you're talking to unbelievers. It calls to mind phrases like "self-righteous" and "holier-than-thou"—a way none of us want to be described. But, as we'll see over the next several sessions, our entire salvation is wrapped up in this word: ***RIGHTEOUSNESS.***

According to verse 17, whose righteousness is revealed?

And that is Paul's big point—salvation is all about God's righteousness, not ours. Next session we'll see why we so desperately need God's righteousness, but for now, Paul was concerned with where righteousness comes from. One of the problems in the Roman church was that some Jewish believers claimed a person's righteousness came through the Law—having it and obeying it. As the ones to whom the Law was originally given, they believed they were more righteous than their Gentile brothers and sisters in Christ. Paul is going to shatter this belief. But first:

> What are some ways, other than faith in Jesus, someone might try to be right with God?

> Name two to three mercies you have seen in our passage this session.

> As we wrap up our first session of study together, try to say your memory verses three times without looking. I promise that memorizing Scripture will benefit you for years to come.

I've so enjoyed spending this time with you. May God, in His great mercy, give us all a greater hunger for His Word, love for His Son, and gratitude for our salvation.

DIGGING DEEPER
Check out these verses to help you better understand today's passage:
Psalm 40:9-12 • 2 Corinthians 5:21 • Philippians 3:8-9

Session Two: IT'S ALL ABOUT THE GOSPEL

WATCH Session Two video teaching.

1. Paul was set apart for the gospel.

_____

_____

_____

_____

_____

2. The church is to be united by the gospel.

_____

_____

_____

_____

_____

3. Paul began his letter with the core of the gospel.

_____

_____

_____

_____

_____

DISCUSSION QUESTIONS

1   What day of personal study had the most impact on you? Why?

2   How did what you heard on the video teaching clarify, reinforce, or give new insight to what you studied this session?

3   What were the important aspects you included in your description of the gospel?

4   How did studying Paul's conversion encourage you?

5   In what ways have you experienced being loved by God, being called by God, and being made (more and more) holy by God?

6   What new mercies did you see in the passage this session?

7   What is the most significant thing you learned about God, the gospel, or yourself this session?

To access the video teaching sessions, use the instructions in the back of your Bible study book.

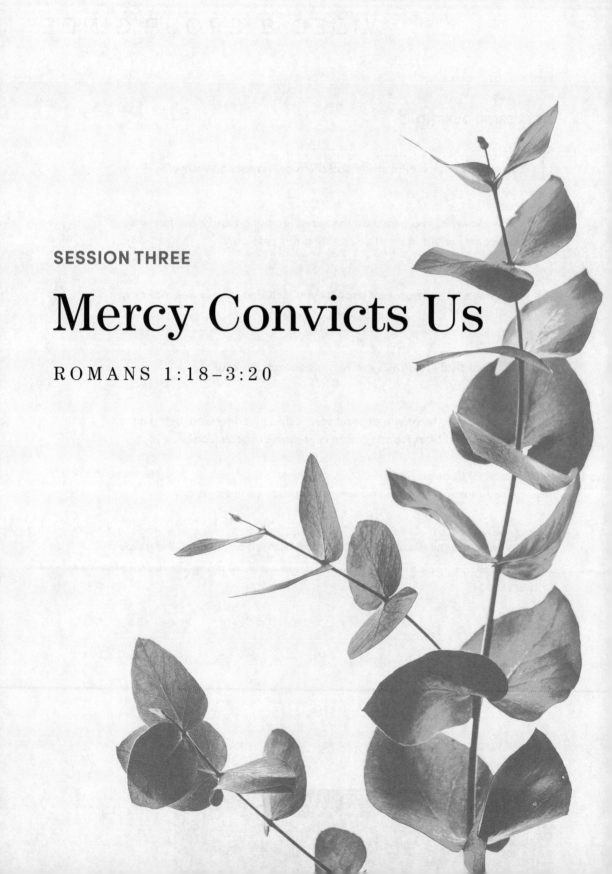

SESSION THREE

Mercy Convicts Us

ROMANS 1:18–3:20

Introduction

Imagine a scenario with me. A friend approaches you, eager and excited to share her good news. She grabs your arm, pulls you aside, and tells you she has just finished multiple rounds of life-saving chemotherapy. As you rejoice with her, she begins to say that you, too, should receive this chemotherapy. She rationalizes that if chemotherapy has been lifesaving for her, it will be so for you, also.

Most of us would think she was crazy. Someone only needs chemotherapy if she has cancer. But how would the scenario change if, the day before you saw your friend, your doctor told you that you had advanced, aggressive cancer throughout your body? With the reality of the diagnosis, I imagine you would become much more interested in the treatment that saved your friend's life.

If we're not sick—or don't know we are—we have no reason to seek a cure. It's never fun to hear a diagnosis. But without one, we won't seek lifesaving treatment.

In our passages this session, Paul was acting like a caring physician, spelling out our sickness. Like any diagnosis, it's hard to hear. But Paul was actually showing us the depths of God's mercy. He knew we would need to hear how desperate our condition is so that we're ready to receive the glorious cure offered to us in the gospel.

MEMORY VERSE

. . . as it is written: "None is righteous, no, not one."

ROMANS 3:10

Prayer for the Week

Father, I bow before You as I open Your Word.

You are good and Your Word is true. Holy Spirit,

open my eyes to see the reality of who I am

apart from You. Remind me how desperately

I need You and show me even greater

depths of Your saving mercy as I study

this week. In Jesus' name, **Amen.**

DAY 1

RIGHTEOUS WRATH

READ ROMANS 1:18-32.

As you begin your study today, ask God to help you move slowly through the text with a heart willing to hear what He has to say.

What Does It Say?

According to Romans 1:17, what was revealed? What is being revealed according to verse 18? Why (against what)?

Theologian John Stott imagined Paul answering a series of questions the reader might raise. His hypothetical conversation goes something like this:

Paul:	*I'm not ashamed of the gospel* (16a).
Q:	Why not, Paul?
Paul:	Because *it is the power of God for the salvation of everyone who believes* (16b).
Q:	How so, Paul?
Paul:	Because *in the gospel, a righteousness from God is revealed* . . . (17).
Q:	But why is this necessary, Paul?
Paul:	Because *the wrath of God is revealed from heaven against all ungodliness and unrighteousness of men, who by their unrighteousness suppress the truth* (18).
Q:	But how have people suppressed the truth, Paul?
Paul:	Because *what may be known about God is plain to them . . . For since the creation of the world God's invisible qualities . . . have been clearly seen* (19-20).[1]

**FOR FURTHER
READING**
Holier than Thou
by Jackie Hill Perry

Thinking about God's wrath can be uncomfortable for us. We'd rather picture God as a benevolent grandpa or, even better, a slightly forgetful Santa Claus—one who chuckles at our mistakes, puts no one on his naughty list, and grants everything on our wish lists. But that's not who our God is.

God is holy. He is perfect in His goodness, His judgment, His righteousness, and His wrath. His wrath is not like ours. Revenge, desire to harm, or pride never fuel God's wrath. It's not arbitrary, hormonal, or resentful. God ultimately pours out His wrath on everything that harms us—evil, sin, unrighteousness, and wickedness—and on everyone who embraces and embodies those things.

A CLOSER LOOK
Three times Paul wrote that "God gave them over" (Rom. 1:24,26,28, NIV). We should tremble at the thought. It means that God will, as a response to continued rebellion and open idolatry, release people to the misery of who we all are apart from Him. This is not God rejecting people. This is God releasing those who persist in rejecting Him. Is there hope for those God gives over? Yes! Because God doesn't give up. He gives people over in hope that they will realize the desperation of their situation and, like the prodigal son, come running back.

Last session we saw that the righteous will live by faith (Rom. 1:17). Today we read that the unrighteous will receive God's wrath (v. 18) and deserve to die (v. 32). Obviously, we want to be counted as one of the righteous. But God, out of His great mercy, is going to show us to which group we actually belong. Remember, in order to embrace the cure, we need the diagnosis.

Three times Paul said, "God gave them up" (or "delivered them over," CSB). Make a list of the sins chronicled as a result.

Verses 24-25:

Verses 26-27:

Verses 28-32:

What Does It Mean?

The main point of our passage today is that the wrath of God is going to be poured out on all the unrighteous—and that He is right to do so. God has revealed Himself and people have rejected Him. The unrighteous are known by their unbelief, which causes them to reject God, suppress the truth, and live unrighteously. They don't believe He is wise and His ways are right. And because of their unbelief, God gave them up.

The resulting sins God gave them over to are lustful impurity (vv. 24-25), homosexuality (vv. 26-27), and the more pervasive effects of general unrighteousness (vv. 28-32). Most of us want to suppress the truth of at least one of the groupings he gave. We either refuse to believe the things listed in verses 24-25 and 26-27 are actually sin, or we minimize the list of sins given in verses 29-31—covetousness, envy, gossip, slander, boastfulness, disobedience to parents— telling ourselves these things surely couldn't cause God's wrath to fall on us.

FOR FURTHER READING
Gay Girl, Good God by Jackie Hill Perry

The current cultural tide pushes us to embrace the thought that "love is love" and all expressions of love are good and right—homosexual, heterosexual, multisexual, before marriage, or outside of marriage. In fact, some of you might be very uncomfortable with these verses. Maybe your first reaction was to dismiss Paul's words, claiming that the situation in Rome was different from our current moment. Or possibly the verses about same-sex relationships describe you or someone you love, and it would be costly to believe that God considers homosexual sex unrighteous. If so, hang in there. Remember, part of belief is trusting that God has the right to determine what is righteous and what is unrighteous— not to condemn, but to convict and save.

Was there anything listed in this passage that you found hard to categorize as unrighteousness? Explain. Do you think some of the listed sins are more deserving of God's wrath than others? Explain. In what ways does the list humble you?

What do you think it means to suppress the truth?

Paul wrote in verse 20 that we "are without excuse." List three to five excuses we use to suppress the truth of what God says about sin. As you think about the sins listed in our passage, which excuses are you most likely to use?

I'm confident we all identify with at least one thing listed in those verses. This was Paul's first step in showing us we all stand in the same place—justly deserving of God's righteous wrath.

However, regardless of the type of sin, we tend to suppress the gravity of it or minimize its seriousness. We lighten its weight by calling sin a mistake, or we blame it on our personality or family of origin, thinking it's just the way we are. We rationalize it as no big deal or attribute it to a difficult or stressful season in life. We easily shift the blame to others. The reality is we suppress the truth of what God says about sin in order to continue doing what we want.

What Do I Do?

Paul stated we are without excuse because everyone, every day, can clearly see God's existence, power, and glory in His creation. Whenever I read those words, I envision a particular scene.

My in-laws lived in Evergreen, Colorado, a town west of Denver on the edge of the Rocky Mountains. When going to visit them, we would drive on I-70 from our home in Kansas to their home. If you've ever driven that stretch of highway, you know that after seven or eight hours of vast, flat, prairie land, the distant shadow of the mountains becomes visible about an hour before you hit Denver. After driving through Denver, the climb through the foothills begins. There is a moment on the journey when you round a bend on I-70 and the Rockies come into full view. The grandeur and vastness of the vista will take your breath away. Everything about this view—the glory, power, majesty, beauty, and creativity—proclaims a Creator.

In what ways have you seen creation reveal our Creator?

According to these verses, what should our response be, and what do we do instead? How have you responded in both right and wrong ways to God's creation?

In every passage we'll study this session, Paul's intent was to show us that the reason God's wrath is righteous is because we all stand hopelessly unrighteous before His perfect holiness. Being confronted with the gravity of our sin can lead us to despair. But the good news—that God has made a way for us to be redeemed—is coming! Paul will get to that, but we need to be prepared to hear it, know why we need it, and be humble enough to gratefully receive it.

Did you read anything in today's passage that convicted you or showed you that you are deserving of God's wrath? If so, how will you respond?

As you work on your memory verse today, let the truth it proclaims sink in. If no one is righteous, then we all justly deserve God's righteous wrath. Don't suppress the truth—let it humble and prepare you.

DIGGING DEEPER
Check out these verses to help you better understand today's passage:
Psalm 19:1 • Psalm 106:19-21 • Colossians 3:5-6

RIGHTEOUS JUDGMENT

READ ROMANS 2:1-11.

As we dive into today's passage, remember that Paul wanted to make sure everyone who's sick receives an accurate diagnosis. He didn't want us to fool ourselves into believing we don't need the cure.

Yesterday, he addressed the unrighteous. Today, he addressed the self-righteous. So if you found yourself eagerly agreeing with Paul's pronouncements of judgment in yesterday's passage, if you felt a touch morally superior to "those people" or grateful you don't struggle with "those sins," today's passage will speak to you. Keep in mind that these confrontational words are meant to be the kindness of God leading us to repentance.

What Does It Say?

> What does God say in Romans 2:1 that he said previously in 1:20? Why do you think He said it twice?

We're so prone to make excuses for our sin, often by comparing ourselves and our sins to others and their sins. We comfort ourselves with thoughts like:

- *At least I haven't done that.*
- *Everyone else is doing it.*
- *No one's perfect.*
- *At least I go to church.*

We prop ourselves up by thinking the best of ourselves—and the worst of others. But God abhors moral superiority as much as moral decay. Further, self-righteous thoughts divide God's people and hinder us from reaching out to others.

The church in Rome suffered from division. Two of Paul's purposes in writing this letter were to encourage the unity of the church and compel them to join him on mission. Paul wanted them to be healed of their division so that they would be able to partner with him as he preached the gospel to the ends of the earth. If a church is not unified, if there is an us-versus-them mentality, or if some feel morally superior to others, how will that church be outward-focused enough to reach the lost? They won't. We won't! Paul began to address the disunity in Rome by showing why they had no basis for self-righteousness or moral superiority.

> **What do you learn about judges, judgment, and judging in Romans 2:1-4? How would you describe the judgment we give versus the judgment God gives?**

As John Stott said, "The underlying theme of this [passage], then, is the judgment of God upon self-appointed judges."[2] We've all done it—appointed ourselves as the judges and arbitrators of what is right and what is wrong. We rank sins in a hierarchy—with ours at the bottom of the list, of course, and "their sins" at the top. We determine who's "in" and who's "out."

Far more often than I care to admit, I give myself abundant grace, but I am stingy with it for others. If I speak harshly or answer someone in anger, I tell myself it's because I'm tired, I have a lot on my mind, or I'm "just a bit grumpy." But if someone else speaks harshly or answers me in anger, I silently think she's unkind, she lacks self-control, or she's not being very godly. In doing so, I've set myself up as the judge of our hearts. But, like Paul said, I only condemn myself because I practice the very thing I condemn in others.

In yesterday's passage, we saw the importance of trusting God to define unrighteousness. Today, we see the importance of trusting Him to judge unrighteousness. As the righteous Judge of all the earth (Gen. 18:25), He does it perfectly.

> **What does Romans 2:2 say about God's judgment? How is His judgment described in verse 5?**

God's judgment is actually a good thing. At some level, we all long for it. Think of the last movie you saw that had a true "bad guy" in it. I'm talking about someone who commits horrible acts and revels in them. What do you want to happen? If you're like me, you want justice. You want the good guy to definitively win and banish the evil person forever. That justice happens as judgment occurs.

Most of us long for justice to prevail—for wrongs to be made right. But justice requires judgment. And it's because God is able to judge faultlessly that God's justice is perfect and His judgments are good.

According to verse 4, what is the intended result of God's kindness?

What Does It Mean?

What three attributes of God are listed in verse 4?

What do you think each one means?

How has God shown each to you?

In what ways might you presume upon each one?

We all sin, but we don't all **REPENT**. Next session we'll discover the good news that God's judgment isn't for the sinner; it's for the *unrepentant* sinner. So if you identify with the morally bankrupt person described in yesterday's passage, the message for you is *repent*. If you see yourself more as the morally superior person in today's passage, the message for you is *repent*. Neither person should despair but rejoice because God shows no partiality and, in His kindness, leads us all to true repentance. Mercy, indeed!

REPENT
Not only confessing our sin to God, but also turning away from it and running toward God and His righteousness.

In verse 11, Paul stated that God shows no partiality or favoritism. How does this help us understand God as a good Judge and His judgment as righteous?

What Do I Do?

Paul asked a very important question in verse 3: *Do you think you will escape the judgment of God?* How would you answer, and what reasons would you give for your answer?

According to verse 5, what prevents people from repenting? What is the result of not repenting? Is there anything you need to repent of today?

Today's passage identifies God alone as the righteous Judge. Our job is not to judge but to repent. As you work on your memory verse today, thank God for His kindness, forbearance, and patience as He leads you toward repentance.

DIGGING DEEPER
Check out these verses to help you better understand today's passage:
Jeremiah 17:10 • Matthew 7:2 • 2 Peter 3:9

RIGHTEOUS WORD

READ ROMANS 2:12-29.

Have you ever heard a statement like this: "Going to church doesn't mean you're a Christian any more than going to a rodeo means you're a cowgirl"? It's true. I've been to a lot of rodeos, even ridden a lot of horses, but no one would call me a cowgirl.

REGENERATION
Literally "re-creation." It's the new birth, the new life, and the new heart that God graciously gives His children.

In the same way, while all Christians should go to church, not all who do go to church are Christians. "Religious" people—people who go through the spiritual motions, trusting in outward distinctions (like church attendance, baptism, and financial giving) rather than inward **REGENERATION**—sit in all of our churches. The outward distinctions are important. God wants His people to gather for worship; He commands His children to be baptized, and He desires His people to give financially. But none of these things save us.

That's basically Paul's point in today's passage. If Day One addressed the unrighteous and Day Two the self-righteous, today's passage addresses the externally righteous.

THE LAW
This usually refers to the Law of Moses, the commandments God gave to the nation of Israel through Moses on Mount Sinai. We find most of these laws in Exodus, Leviticus, and Deuteronomy.

Here are some tips that might help us understand and apply his words:

- When Paul talked about someone with (or under) **THE LAW**, he was talking about a Jewish person (because God gave the Jews His Law through Moses).
    - When applying this in our context, we can think about religious or church-going people—some who are true believers and some who are not. They are familiar with the ways and Word of God.

- When Paul talked about someone apart from the Law, he was talking about anyone not Jewish—a Gentile.
    - For our context, we can think about people who are non-religious and don't go to church—those unfamiliar with God's Word and His ways.

What Does It Say?

What are the two categories of people mentioned in verse 13? What does each hope for? Which group receives it?

Both groups are looking to be **JUSTIFIED**, or declared righteous, by God. By this point in the study you've probably realized the idea of righteousness is pretty important. We've read that the gospel reveals God's righteousness (Rom. 1:16-17) and that His wrath is being poured out on all unrighteousness and self-righteousness (1:18; 2:2). Now we read it will be the "doers of the law" who will be declared righteous (2:13).

JUSTIFIED
Declared by God to be righteous. It is the opposite of condemnation.

Is that good news or not? If righteousness is what I need, then it looks as if I just need to be a (perfect) doer of the Law. (Spoiler alert: Paul will soon tell us that "by works of the law no human being will be justified in his sight" (3:20)—but we'll get there soon enough.)

Romans 2:13 seems to raise the question: *Can I do enough good things to be saved?* If you've been a believer for a while, you might want to quickly yell, *No, we're saved only by faith in Jesus!* But remember, Paul is making sure we understand the severity of our diagnosis. Can we be saved by our works?

In an attempt to stump his students, seminary professor and theologian Dr. R. C. Sproul used to ask them, "How many ways are there to get into heaven?" After they unanimously responded "One," he would shockingly reply, *No, there are two.* He would point out that one way is through faith in Jesus Christ and the other is by leading a life of perfect obedience and perfect righteousness. He told his students: "If a person lives a life that is in perfect obedience to the law of God, they don't need Jesus Christ. Jesus Christ came to save people who do not live perfect lives. The tragedy is that there are actually people who believe their lives are good enough to get them into heaven."[3]

We all put our hope in something. Many people hope a "good life" will grant them entrance into heaven—trusting the good they do will outweigh the bad. Others place their hope in religious activity, such as church attendance, faithful participation in Bible study, or affiliation with the "right" denomination.

Read Romans 2:17-27 and list everything the Jewish Christians in Rome were putting their hope in.

What Does It Mean?

Read Matthew 5:21-22,27-28. How does Jesus' teaching help us understand Paul's words in Romans 2:21-22?

Why do you think the boasting listed in verses 17–23 caused "the name of God [to be] blasphemed among the Gentiles" (v. 24)? In what ways do we do the same thing today with the same effect?

Read Ezekiel 36:23,26-27.

According to verses 26–27, list what God promised to do.

According to these verses, what do you think God desires?

What similarities do you see with Romans 2:28–29?

God is not unconcerned with our outward behavior or our outward obedience. But our obedience never causes our salvation; it's the result of it. Being a good person will never save us. Neither will religious activity. Only a new heart of flesh—a "circumcised heart"— given by God, allows us to obey in a way that pleases God. Our external righteousness, our good deeds, and our obedience are not the root of our salvation, but the glorious fruit.

What Do I Do?

For those who've walked with the Lord for a while, have you ever felt pride over knowing exactly where to flip in your Bible to find Habakkuk or Philemon? Do you feel pride right now that you know what those books are? What about pride over knowing the right answer to a Bible trivia question. Yes? Me too.

Have you ever felt pride because your granddaddy was a preacher, or your parents helped build the church you now worship in, or you serve in some church leadership capacity? Do you have an underlying sense that these things indicate a greater righteousness? Do you think your spiritual heritage or religious résumé makes you more pleasing to God than the person of whom none of the above is true? This passage addresses all of us who answered yes to any of these questions.

> At the end of the day, most of us want to be right with God. List four to five things you could be tempted to put your hope in for that right relationship.

> Paul told his readers that those with a circumcised heart—who become not just hearers, but doers of the Law—will be right with God. What evidence can you offer that you've been given a heart of flesh, that you are a Christian not "merely one outwardly . . . [but] one inwardly . . . by the Spirit" (vv. 28-29)?

> If your list consists of only religious activity—going to church, being baptized, tithing—and not the things that spring from the obedience of faith, then run to the Lord. Repent and tell Him that you need a heart of flesh, and He will be faithful to give you one.

> If you can point to evidence of a new life, a new heart, and a new birth, rejoice and write a prayer of thanksgiving to the One who saved you.

The big question continues to come at us: *How can I be right with God?* The answer will burst onto the scene next session. But for now, rejoice that Jesus can give the unrighteous, the self-righteous, and the externally righteous new hearts. Work on your memory verse and hope in Jesus!

DIGGING DEEPER
Check out these verses to help you better understand today's passage:
Jeremiah 31:33 • Matthew 7:1-5 • James 1:22-25

RIGHTEOUS WAYS

READ ROMANS 3:1-8.

Yesterday we noted that some people who go to church aren't true believers. Your church has some. My church has some. You may be one. Here's the question before us: *Is there any benefit for those people?* To use Paul's words, "Much in every way" (v. 2)!

What Does It Say?

Paul wrote these verses as if he were in a debate. He imagined an opponent, someone who questioned him at every turn. Paul predicted the objections that would be raised.

> **What are the first two questions the imaginary objector raised (v. 1), and how did Paul answer them?**

> **What are the next two questions (v. 3), and how did Paul answer?**

> **What question is posed in verse 5, and how did Paul answer?**

I used to teach a class on parenting. One evening, about halfway through the class, a childcare worker knocked on the door and entered. I smiled and stopped talking, knowing she was there to pull some poor unsuspecting parent out of class to go deal with his or her child's naughty behavior. But she looked at me and said, "Can you come with me? We're having a hard time with your child."

I excused myself (somewhat sheepishly), followed her, talked with my child, dealt out the discipline, and headed back to class. Understandably, the class wanted to know what I did.

I shared with them the actions I took. Several in the class commended and praised me for my "patience, wisdom, and follow-through."

I'm not telling you this story so you'll think I was a great parent. My purpose is to ask what you would think if, on the way home from church that night, my child had said to me, "Well, I'm assuming I won't get in trouble. After all, my disobedience ended up bringing you much praise. My rebellion made you look good. You're welcome."

That is the ridiculous argument Paul was combatting—that God should be grateful for our unrighteousness because it highlights His glorious righteousness. By no means!

What Does It Mean?

> When Paul spoke of God's faithfulness in verse 3, what do you think he was referring to?

Several hundred years before Jesus was born, the Jewish people had been exiled from the promised land. Some were killed, many suffered, most lost everything. One scholar wrote, "These experiences, so contrary to the Jews' expectations about God's . . . faithfulness to them [made them question]. How could God allow his people to suffer? . . . What was he doing? What were his purposes?"[4] Have you ever wondered the same things?

What are your expectations of God's faithfulness? Does the statement "God is faithful" mean God will always "have your back"? That you won't ever suffer? That you won't be unemployed or sick or lonely? That no one will go to hell? The faithfulness of God means that, above all, He is faithful to His Word, His plans, and His purposes. Paul wanted his readers to see that God is being faithful not only when He's patient and kind, but also when He judges sin.

Read the following passage from Nehemiah 9:32-33 and then answer the questions:

> [32]Now, therefore, our God, the great, the mighty, and the awesome God, who keeps covenant and steadfast love, let not all the hardship seem little to you that has come upon us, upon our kings, our princes, our priests, our prophets, our fathers, and all your people, since the time of the kings of Assyria until this day. [33]Yet you have been righteous in all that has come upon us, for you have dealt faithfully and we have acted wickedly.

The Israelites had been unfaithful for centuries. God exiled them from the promised land and then brought them back. How did Nehemiah describe God (v. 32)?

What words did he use to describe God's actions in judging them (v. 33)?

How do these verses support Paul's words in our passage this session?

MEANS OF GOD'S GRACE
The ways God has provided for us to receive and grow in faith—especially His Word, prayer, baptism, Lord's Supper, and fellowship with other believers.

What Do I Do?

Circle back to the question asked in the first paragraph, *What benefit is there for the unbeliever in being around the Word of God?* Imagine an unbelieving child or spouse attending church regularly with his or her family member. Week after week this person hears the Word of God preached, contemplates the meaning of the Lord's Supper, watches baptisms, and hears prayers. These are all **MEANS OF GOD'S GRACE** to us. They're effective. God uses them to draw us, convict us, instruct us, and point us to salvation. It's better to be unsaved and in church than unsaved and not in church. Both groups need Jesus, but the first has a greater opportunity to encounter Him.

Make a list of every benefit you experience by:

Going to church

Reading your Bible

Being baptized

Receiving the Lord's Supper

In Romans 3:4, Paul quoted the words of David from Psalm 51: "That you may be justified in your words, and prevail when you are judged." David had committed adultery with Bathsheba, had her husband killed, and tried to cover up the whole thing. God confronted David through the prophet Nathan. David immediately repented and, at some point later, penned these words, "Against you, you only, have I sinned and done what is evil in your sight, so that you may be justified in your words and blameless in your judgment" (Ps. 51:4). David was saying that God was right in judging him. God was not acting against His character but was faithful to it. But because David also knew that God is loving, gracious, and merciful, David repented and called out for God's forgiveness and restoration.

Read Psalm 51. How did David's words indicate true repentance? Is there anything you need to repent of? Use these words from Psalm 51 as a prayer of repentance. Join David in knowing that God hears, God forgives, and God restores.

Purge me with hyssop, and I shall be clean;
wash me, and I shall be whiter than snow.
Let me hear joy and gladness;
let the bones that you have broken rejoice.
Hide your face from my sins,
and blot out all my iniquities.
Create in me a clean heart, O God,
and renew a right spirit within me.
Cast me not away from your presence,
and take not your Holy Spirit from me.
Restore to me the joy of your salvation,
and uphold me with a willing spirit.

PSALM 51:7-12

As you work on your memory verse today, thank God for His means of grace that both convict and strengthen you. He is always faithful.

DIGGING DEEPER
Check out these verses to help you better understand today's passage:
Psalm 7:11 • Psalm 98:3 • Hebrews 4:12

NO ONE IS RIGHTEOUS

READ ROMANS 3:9-20.

All week we've been looking at our passages through the lens of a physician's diagnosis. Let's switch for a moment from a doctor's office to a courtroom. Today's verses are like the closing arguments in an open-and-shut case that Paul's been arguing since Romans 1:18. The question is, *Who can stand before the Judge and be declared righteous (i.e. innocent)?* Paul began with the unrighteous and concluded they are all under wrath and without excuse (1:20). Paul then moved on to the self-righteous and the externally religious people, declaring they, too, are both without excuse. In fact, the things they cling to in hopes of offering a defense do the exact opposite—condemn, not exonerate (2:1).

Paul anticipated every objection and presented an airtight case. From even the people who might have thought they were the exceptions to the rule to the ones who couldn't identify with any of the sins listed up until this point, there was no disputing Paul's final declaration: "None is righteous, no, not one" (3:10).

What Does It Say?

According to verses 9-12, answer the following questions:

Who is under sin?	
Who is righteous?	
Who understands God?	
Who seeks for God?	
Who have turned aside?	
Who does good?	

According to verses 19-20, what is the result of this indictment, and who will be justified?

When Paul said "that every mouth may be stopped," he was saying the case is over (v. 19). No more arguments or excuses. No chance of acquittal. No place for a plea bargain. God's verdict is *guilty*; His sentence is *death*, and His judgment is both *righteous* and *just*. From this moment on, the guilty (everyone, including you and me) are placed on death row, awaiting our final execution.

What Does It Mean?

What do you think it means to be "under sin" (v. 9)? How is that different from committing a sin? How does this phrase help us understand humanity's greatest need?

To be "under sin" is to be under its dominion, its rule. Paul wanted his readers to understand that sin is an oppressive tyrant that crushes us under its cruel weight. (More on this in a few sessions.) We are unable to throw this tyrant off. We need Someone who is not "under sin"—Someone strong enough and good enough—to rescue us from the domain of sin.

Why do you think Paul used so many words describing sins of the tongue (vv. 13-14)? How does Luke 6:45 help us answer this question?

Because Romans 3:20 is so important, I want you to read it in three translations:

> For no one will be justified in his sight by the works of the law, because the knowledge of sin comes through the law (CSB).

> For by works of the law no human being will be justified in his sight, since through the law comes knowledge of sin (ESV).

> Therefore no one will be declared righteous in God's sight by the works of the law; rather, through the law we become conscious of our sin (NIV).

Using our definitions for *justified* (p. 47) and *righteous* (p. 30), rewrite this verse in your own words and make it personal by inserting your name.

What Do I Do?

What is your status in our imaginary courtroom? Do you have any objections to offer God in your defense? Or are you standing quietly because your mouth has been stopped by the truth of God's Word? Describe what it feels like to stand guilty before the righteous Judge.

In three to five sentences, summarize what you have learned this session. Where have you seen God's mercy?

The judgment has been handed down and the verdict is in: Guilty. The sentence: Death. Or if we were to return to the doctor's office, we would say the diagnosis has been given. *Terminal with a 0% chance of survival.* The bad news is really bad. The temptation to run ahead, jump to the good news, is real. But don't. Allow the truth of our condition to settle deeper into your soul.

As we end this session, reflect on these lyrics from the hymn "Rock of Ages, Cleft for Me"

> Not the labors of my hands
> can fulfill thy law's demands;
> could my zeal no respite know,
> could my tears forever flow,
> all for sin could not atone;
> thou must save, and thou alone.
>
> Nothing in my hand I bring,
> simply to the cross I cling;
> naked, come to thee for dress;
> helpless, look to thee for grace;
> foul, I to the fountain fly;
> wash me, Savior, or I die.[5]

And that is where we are: *Jesus—wash me, heal me, acquit me, save me—or I die.*

DIGGING DEEPER
Check out these verses to help you better understand today's passage:
Psalm 9:9-10 • Psalm 14:2-3 • John 3:18

Session Three: NO ONE RIGHTEOUS

WATCH Session Three video teaching.

1. Sin is real.

_____

_____

_____

_____

_____

_____

2. Sin is universal.

_____

_____

_____

_____

_____

_____

3. Sin is serious.

_____

_____

_____

_____

_____

_____

VIDEO & GROUP GUIDE

DISCUSSION QUESTIONS

1   What day of personal study had the most impact on you? Why?

2   How did what you heard on the video teaching clarify, reinforce, or give new insight to what you studied this session?

3   In what ways is conviction of sin a mercy?

4   Do you think some of the sins are more deserving of God's wrath than others? Explain.

5   What do you think it means to be "under sin" (Rom. 3:9)? How is that different from committing a sin? How does this phrase help us understand humanity's greatest need?

6   What new mercies did you see in the passage this session?

7   What is the most significant thing you learned about God, the gospel, or yourself this session?

To access the video teaching sessions, use the instructions in the back of your Bible study book.

SESSION FOUR

Mercy Saves Us

ROMANS 3:21–4:25

Introduction

Oh, friends, my heart has been so eager to get to this session! We ended last session sitting on death row, justly accused, deserving of God's righteous indictment, without hope of a last-minute acquittal. He cannot turn a blind eye to sin. The sentence is severe but not unjust. The punishment is punitive but not unfair. Our sins rightly condemn us.

However (and praise God for this however!), the righteous Judge is also merciful. Because His mercy extends beyond our wildest imaginations, He did the unimaginable. He sent His only Son, His perfectly innocent and righteous Son, into the courtroom to stand before the bench. The Son turned to you and to me and offered us the great exchange. In essence, He said, "I will take your sentence, and you take my righteousness. You may go free, receive my status—not guilty, righteous—and live. And I will take your sentence—condemnation and death. I will substitute Myself for you." Who would say no to such mercy?

This is the unfathomable gift of the gospel. Oh friend, rejoice with me at the mercy of God. If you have not accepted this incomprehensible offer, today would be a great day to do so. Thank the righteous Judge for His mercy and praise the Son that His righteousness can be yours through faith.

MEMORY VERSES

> But now the righteousness of God has been manifested apart from the law, although the Law and the Prophets bear witness to it—the righteousness of God through faith in Jesus Christ for all who believe. For there is no distinction.

ROMANS 3:21-22

Prayer for the Week

Father, Son, and Holy Spirit, I bow before You and praise You for Your incomprehensible mercy. Thank You that You love me and came to rescue me. As I study Your Word this week, open my eyes to see greater depths of Your mercy. Help me rest more in the work of Your great salvation. And open my heart that I might love You more with all that I am and all that I do. In Jesus' matchless name, **Amen.**

CHRIST ALONE

READ ROMANS 3:21-26.

Some say that Romans 3:21-26 is "the most essential paragraph in the most essential book of the Bible."[1] Dr. Leon Morris called it "possibly the most important single paragraph ever written."[2] Go back and read it again. Read it out loud if possible. Commit to your memory work this week—these verses contain magnificent truths to hide in your heart.

What Does It Say?

Paul mentioned God's righteousness four times in this passage. List what you learn about God's righteousness in each reference.

According to verse 22:

What is given?

By what means?

To whom?

According to verse 25, who put Jesus forward? For what purpose?

Some of your Bibles might say *propitiation*; others might say *mercy seat* or *sacrifice of atonement*. All mean that God poured every ounce of His wrath toward sin onto Jesus, the perfect sacrifice, on the cross. The wrath we deserve was fully spent on Jesus.

A verse of the popular Christian song "In Christ Alone" spells it out. Google® the lyrics to "In Christ Alone" and write the words that clearly depict this truth.

The Sacrifice that satisfied was sent by His Father. The Son came willingly, submissively, and perfectly. As one scholar said, "God's righteousness provides what God's righteousness requires."[3] Mercy indeed.

What Does It Mean?

We will never be righteous by obeying the Law because we can never obey it perfectly. Our only hope is for a righteousness that comes from somewhere else. And in His great mercy, God provided a righteousness "apart from the law" (v. 21).

Most of us have heard (and affirm) that salvation is:

- in Christ alone;

- through faith alone;

- by grace alone.

Where do you see the truth of each statement in these verses?

What difference does being "justified freely by his grace" make (v. 24, CSB)? What would the opposite be?

What do we learn about God in verse 26? Thinking about our courtroom scene from the introduction, how can God be both just and the One who justifies?

This is the heart of God—utterly holy and wholly merciful. His holiness cannot tolerate sin. But His mercy compels Him to rescue sinners. In His infinite wisdom, He has put forth a way that satisfies both His justice and His love. But don't ever think the problem of our sin was easy to rectify. It wasn't. As Dr. Cornelius Plantinga wrote:

> Christians have always measured sin, in part, by the suffering needed to atone for it. The ripping and writhing of a body on a cross, the bizarre metaphysical maneuver of using death to defeat death, the urgency of the summons to human beings to ally themselves with the events of Christ and with the person of these events, and then to make that person and those events the center of their lives—these things tell us that the main human trouble is desperately difficult to fix, even for God, and that sin is the longest-running of human emergencies.[4]

God Himself went to immeasurable and inscrutable lengths to simultaneously punish the sin and forgive the sinner.

What are the similarities between these verses (vv. 21-22) and your memory verses from Session Two (1:16-17)? What new information are we given?

How do these verses show that "there is salvation in no one else, for there is no other name under heaven given among men by which we must be saved" (Acts 4:12)?

What Do I Do?

Our verses today are not about what we can do—but about what God has done. Salvation is not a joint partnership where we do our part and God does His. It's not as if we run as far or climb as high as we can and then God carries us the rest of the way. No! The only thing we contribute to our salvation is the sin that necessitates it.[5]

So instead of trying to earn your salvation or merit God's favor, I want to encourage you to respond in one of two ways. If you belong to Jesus and have received His righteousness by faith, then pray through the verses we've studied today, thanking God for doing everything necessary for your salvation.

If you do not yet belong to Jesus, I tell you with the utmost love that you stand in the most horrible place possible—condemned, unrighteous, and defenseless before a holy God, our righteous Judge. But the good news is that you don't have to stay there. You can experience the great exchange! Ask God to give you the faith to believe that Jesus' righteousness can be yours right now. If you repent and place faith in Jesus, you can be declared righteous and forgiven of every (yes, every) sin you have ever committed. You can be set free from guilt and condemnation. To paraphrase John 3:16:

> For God so loved _____ (insert your name), that He gave His only
> Son, so that if you believe in Him you will not perish but have eternal life.

Write your prayer of response to God.

DIGGING DEEPER
Check out these verses to help you better understand today's passage:
Acts 4:11-12 • Ephesians 1:7-8 • 2 Timothy 1:8-10

FAITH ALONE

READ ROMANS 3:27-31.

If I ever climb Mount Kilimanjaro, you can bet your bottom dollar that I will literally shout it from the mountaintop—maybe even that one. Climbing a mountain of that size and level of difficulty is an admirable feat. I doubt anyone would deny me my bragging rights. But if I reached the top only because someone carried me the whole way, do you think I would brag? Absolutely! But not about myself. I would boast about the one who carried me.

This is Paul's point. When you receive something you did not earn, why in the world would you boast as if you had achieved it on your own?

What Does It Say?

What happens to our boasting (v. 27)? Why?

Benjamin Franklin famously said, "In reality, there is, perhaps, no one of our natural passions so hard to subdue as *pride*. Disguise it, struggle with it, beat it down, stifle it, mortify it as much as one pleases, it is still alive . . . for, even if I could conceive that I had completely overcome it, I should probably be proud of my humility."[6] Isn't that the truth? Boasting is the native language of our sinful soul.

So far in Paul's letter to the Romans, we've seen that we can't boast in our righteousness because we have none. We can't boast in our religiosity because it's empty. We can't boast in our obedience to the Law because we fail at every point. What remains for us to boast in?

What word appears five times in this passage? What do you learn about it?

We will learn a lot more about faith in the coming weeks, but for now, we need to know that faith is simply the conduit through which God's righteousness comes to us. We are saved *through* faith, not *because* of our faith.

Ironically, far too many Christians place more faith in their faith than in the object of their faith. We hear (or say), "God will heal/provide/act if my faith is just strong enough." God is under no obligation to act if we can just somehow muster a strong enough faith. One commentator compared our faith to nothing more than a rusty, dented, cheap metal ring that holds the clasp of the priceless jewel of Jesus.[7]

Our faith doesn't have to be strong. It's the object of our faith, Jesus, who is strong. Our faith is not magnificent. Jesus is. Our faith is not noteworthy. Jesus is. We don't boast in our faith. We boast in Jesus Christ. The value is not in our faith but in the One to whom our faith, by grace, allows us to hold onto. Faith is merely the clasp that holds the precious jewel of Christ.

What Does It Mean?

God does not play favorites. He has no bias or prejudice. But God's people do, and we see it in the Roman church. Some of the Jewish Christians thought they were God's favorites (not that He didn't *accept* the Gentiles, just that He probably *preferred* the Jews). Paul put that thought to death for them and left no room for us to boast either.

> According to verses 29-30, what does God do and how?

> What do you think the phrase "since God is one" (or "since there is one God," CSB) has to do with Paul's argument (v. 30)?

> Describe how both Jewish and Gentile Christians in the church in Rome might have felt when they read verses 29-30.

Lastly, Paul addressed our relationship with the Law. He already established we'll never be declared right with God by obeying the Law. The next logical question should be, *Then do we just pitch the Law out?* Or we could also ask, *Since I'm saved by grace, do I still need to obey God's Word?*

> **According to verses 29–31, how would you describe what the Law can and cannot do? What does it mean to uphold the Law?**

The Law of God is good, but, as we've already seen, it cannot save us. However, the question Paul was answering revolved around what the relationship between the Christian—the person who has already been saved by grace—and the Law should be. His answer? Uphold it.

The Christian should love God's Law. In the Law we learn how to love God and love others. In it, we're reminded of God's great love for us. The Law imparts wisdom and joy. It is meant to be a delight to our souls and a light for our paths (Ps. 119:105).

Read Psalm 19:7-11 and write down everything the Law does.

What Do I Do?

The gospel is meant to humble and unite us—not because it does away with our differences, but because it celebrates them. God gloriously saves people from every language and nation, men and women, old and young, rich and poor, brown, black, white, and every shade in-between. He does not favor any one type of people over another. The question is, *do you?*

Do you ever think that your nationality, family history, church attendance, Bible knowledge, morality, education, age, self-awareness, social engagement, cultural activism, political party, social connections, financial portfolio, spiritual gifts, or other factors place you in a superior position to others?

> **If so, in which of the above are you most tempted to boast? In which of the above are you most tempted to feel superior to others?**

Every good thing we have—our faith, our justification, our ethnicity, our education, the color of our skin, our callings, our gifts, even our obedience—is a gift from God (Jas. 1:17). This should exclude all boasting, engender deep humility, and unite God's people.

> Write a prayer, boasting in Jesus and all He has done to save you. Ask Him to humble you, do away with any boasting, and unite you with all your brothers and sisters in Christ.

> As you work on your memory verses for this week, rejoice that righteousness and faith have been given to you for your salvation.

DIGGING DEEPER
Check out these verses to help you better understand today's passage:
1 Corinthians 1:28-31 • Galatians 3:8-9 • Ephesians 2:8-9

GRACE ALONE

READ ROMANS 4:1-8.

So far, we've sat in a hypothetical doctor's office to hear our diagnosis, and we've stood in a theoretical courtroom to receive our verdict. Today we're going to visit an imaginary accountant and receive some astonishingly good—and true—news. Your spiritual account has been credited with something you did not earn.

What Does It Say?

According to verses 1–8, answer the following:

What did Abraham receive?

What did he do to receive it?

How did he receive it? What action did God take?

Besides Abraham, what other man is mentioned in this passage? What did Paul say about both of them in regard to works?

Genesis 12–25 tells the story of Abraham, the father of the Jewish nation. God entered into covenant with Abraham (Gen. 12; 15; 17), gave him the sign of circumcision (Gen. 17), and promised him, well, the promised land. Abraham lived a life that featured moments of astonishing obedience (Gen. 12; 22) as well as moments of profound failure (Gen. 12; 16; 20).

The story of David, the second king of Israel, is told in 1–2 Samuel. He was the king to whom all the other kings were compared and called "a man after [God's] own heart" (1 Sam 13:14). God entered into covenant with David and promised him his offspring would have an everlasting throne and kingdom (2 Sam. 7). David was a warrior, a psalmist, a great king—as well as an adulterer, liar, and murderer.

> What does God count or credit in Romans 4:3,5–6? What does he not count or credit in verse 8?

Both Abraham and David were heroes of the faith. And both men failed miserably. When Paul wrote that Abraham was not justified because of his works, he was stating that good works don't save any of us—not even the father of our faith. And when he mentioned David, who was justified apart from, or in spite of, his works, he was saying that even our sin doesn't thwart our salvation. Good works don't earn us any credit and bad works (sins) don't discredit believers before God because our sins are forgiven and covered in Christ (v. 7).

What Does It Mean?

> In light of what we've studied so far in Romans, what is the significance of verse 3? What difference would it make if Abraham had been declared righteous because of his obedience or good deeds?

> What is each of the following contrasted with in this passage?
>
> Works:
>
> Wages:

Paul was using the language of accounting. If cash is credited to my bank account, one of two things has happened. Either I've earned the money by working for it (wages, pay), or I've received the money as a gift.

Paul said the same holds true in regard to righteousness and salvation. Either I earn it (like wages) through good deeds—in which case God owes me because I've worked for it. Or I simply receive it as a gift freely given. The difference between my bank account and salvation, however, is that earning righteousness is not an option. Paul has already told us that no one is righteous, and all our attempts to be righteous are in vain. So the credit either comes by grace as a gift or it does not come at all.

What Do I Do?

Which is harder for you to believe—that your good works don't earn you any credit with God or that your bad works (sins) don't count against you if you are in Christ? Explain. How do these verses help you stop striving to earn what God gives freely and begin to rest in what God has already done for you?

Paul quoted Psalm 32:1-2 in verses 7-8. Read the entire psalm, remembering David and his great sins against the Lord. Then, using this psalm as a template, write a similar prayer of response expressing your joy over God's forgiveness and salvation.

Romans 4:1-8 is full of good news. We don't have to strive or fear. We don't have to wonder if we've done enough—or sinned too much. We can rest because God alone has accomplished our salvation. Out of His great mercy, God credits our account with something we desperately need, could never earn, and most certainly don't deserve—the righteousness of Christ. And because we don't earn it, we can never lose it! All that is required of us is that we believe—and even that is a gift. So, sister, rest. If you believe "in him who justifies the ungodly," your sins are covered, and you have been counted as righteous before God (v. 5). Blessing indeed.

DIGGING DEEPER
Check out these verses to help you better understand today's passage:
Genesis 15:1-6 • John 8:39-40 • Galatians 3:5-7

GRACE COMES FIRST

READ ROMANS 4:9-12.

The boarding process of most commercial airlines can be a strange experience. I've never understood why airlines don't board the people sitting in the back of the plane first and then simply continue boarding from back to front until the whole plane is full. Not only would following that process eliminate squeezing past knees and luggage, but it would also do away with those awkward few moments where those sitting in the less expensive coach seats walk past those sitting in the first-class seats. It's an odd social dynamic—a modern day example of the "haves" and the "have-nots." You're all on the same plane, but with a clear line of social delineation.

The church in Rome experienced a similar dynamic. Even though, at some level, the Jewish Christians understood everyone was on the same "plane," many of them viewed themselves as the ones sitting in first class, while the Gentile Christians were the ones sitting in coach. Paul said the righteousness of God was available for all who believe (Rom. 3:22) and God was the God of both Jews and the Gentiles (3:29). But they had difficulty believing they didn't hold a special status before the Lord.

What Does It Say?

In Romans 4:9-12, what two groups did Paul identify?

CIRCUMCISION
The physical act of removing the foreskin of all eight-day old male Israelite children, commanded by God in Genesis 17 as a sign of participation in God's covenant people.

Remember one of the problems the church in Rome faced was lack of unity between the Jewish Christians and the Gentile Christians. The Jewish Christians believed, since God gave them the Law, the covenants, the patriarchs, and **CIRCUMCISION**, they had a special standing, an "in," with God that the Gentiles didn't. This thinking divided the two groups.

Paul had combatted this error earlier in the letter. He said righteousness is not based on having the Word of God but on obeying it. He even said that it's circumcision, not of the flesh, but of the heart that matters. But it seems he felt the need to say it again and again and again. Spiritual pride and moral superiority are hard to kill.

Answer the following questions about the flow of Paul's argument:

What big question did Paul ask (v. 9)?

On what question does his argument hinge (v. 10)?

What is the answer (vv. 10–11)?

What are the two results (vv. 11–12)?

What Does It Mean?

How should Paul's argument have promoted unity in the church in Rome?

According to verse 11, what was the purpose of circumcision?

What does the phrase "walk in the footsteps of the faith that our father Abraham had before he was circumcised" indicate (v. 12)?

At first glance, we might think these verses don't have much to do with us. I'm assuming few of us experience spiritual pride over whether or not our fathers, brothers, nephews, or sons were circumcised. Not many of us claim circumcision as the reason for our salvation.

However, many people throughout the world point to their baptism—the sign and seal of the new covenant—as the substance of their salvation. When asked if they will go to heaven, many will reply, "Yes, I've been baptized."

In the same way that salvation for Abraham was not faith + circumcision, our salvation is not faith + baptism. Circumcision never saved a person. Baptism does not save a person. Everyone is saved the same way—faith alone in Christ alone by grace alone.

What Do I Do?

> What role does your baptism play in your faith? Can someone be saved without being baptized? Why or why not?

Even though circumcision didn't save an Israelite, it was an important step of obedience. If you don't believe me, read Exodus 4:24-26. In the same way, baptism doesn't save, but it is an ordinance given by God that His people do in faith and obedience.

Baptism serves as both a sign and a seal of a spiritual reality. As a sign, baptism is a visible demonstration of an invisible reality. It displays what happened to us when we were born again—we were washed, cleansed, buried, and raised in newness of life.

Baptism serves as a seal in the same way an ancient king's signet ring would seal a letter. The letter was truly from the king without the seal, but the seal authenticated the message the letter contained and guaranteed its contents belonged to the king. As one scholar said, "Circumcision did not *make* Abraham righteous, it *sealed* 'the righteousness that he had by faith while he was still uncircumcised (4:11a).'"[8] Baptism, much like circumcision, serves as an outward seal marking the people who belong to God.

> Do you believe there are different "levels" of Christians? Why or why not? How do these verses help you see the truth?

Paul wanted his readers to know that not even father Abraham held a spiritual first-class ticket. No one does. So, whether you feel you might be one of the spiritual "haves" or you are convinced you are a spiritual "have-not," remember this truth: *We are all in the same kind of seat on the hypothetical plane only because we have a merciful, powerful, kind, forgiving, and gracious God who has placed us there.*

DIGGING DEEPER

Check out these verses to help you better understand today's passage:
Genesis 17:4-7 • Deuteronomy 30:6 • Hebrews 11:8-12

DAY 5

GRACE TO BELIEVE

READ ROMANS 4:13-25.

I don't remember many sermons from my childhood, but one stands out because of an illustration our pastor used. He told the story of a man who strung a tightrope across Niagara Falls. Legend has it that as the crowd gathered, he brought a wheelbarrow to the edge of the falls where the tightrope began. He asked the crowd, "Do you believe I can push this wheelbarrow across this tightrope to the other side?" A few in the crowd said, "Yes," but most were silent. The man successfully pushed the wheelbarrow across the tightrope to the other side. The crowd erupted in cheers. He asked again, "Do you believe I can push this wheelbarrow across this tightrope to the other side?" This time, the whole crowd erupted with a loud, "Yes!" The man successfully accomplished the feat a second time. At this point, a large crowd had gathered. He asked the question a third time, "Do you believe I can push this wheelbarrow across this tightrope to the other side?" Everyone in the crowd yelled, "Yes, we believe!" He then turned to the confident crowd and asked for a volunteer willing to ride in the wheelbarrow. Not one person stepped forward.[9]

We say "I believe" so easily. But true faith requires much more than mere intellectual assent. It involves active trust in and reliance on the object of your faith. As we said earlier, faith itself is not so amazing. What's truly amazing is the One in whom our faith resides.

What Does It Say?

This passage is all about God and the trustworthiness of His Word. To examine it, let's break it into three categories: God, Abraham, and us.

God	Abraham	Us
What did God promise Abraham (v. 13)?	What was Abraham called in verses 16, 17, and 18?	What will be counted (or credited) to us when we believe (v. 24)?
What did grace have to do with the promise (v. 16)?	What convinced Abraham the promise would be fulfilled (vv. 18–21)?	What exactly did Paul tell us to believe (vv. 24–25)?
What two truths about God did Paul highlight (v. 17)?		Why was Jesus delivered over to death (v. 25)?
		Why was He raised to life (v. 25)?

What Does It Mean?

Our passage today is like reading CliffsNotes® for Genesis 12–22! The short version is that God called Abraham to follow Him (which Abraham did) and promised Abraham he would be a great nation (Gen. 12:1-2). God told Abraham He would give Abraham descendants as numerous as the stars in the heavens (Gen. 15:5) and make him the father of a multitude of nations (Gen. 17:5-6). However, there was a slight problem: Abraham was one hundred years old, Sarah, his wife, was ninety, and they still had no children together. It must have been hard for Abraham to believe he would have even one offspring with Sarah, much less innumerable ones.

What does Romans 4:18–21 tell us about how Abraham viewed his situation?

Paul said Abraham did not waver in unbelief but remained fully convinced that God's promise would come to pass. God gave life to Sarah's womb and Abraham's seed. Isaac— the promised offspring—was born. The situation that appeared hopeless wasn't hopeless for God. When God promises, He always fulfills.

What do you think it means to believe in hope against all hope?

What Do I Do?

Abraham's faith was in God's Word, His promises. It resided there because Abraham knew in whom he believed. He was convinced that God was able to accomplish every word God had spoken. This confidence allowed Abraham to hope when everything around him appeared hopeless.

If we want to follow in the footsteps of Abraham's faith (v. 12), then we have to know God's Word. We have to know which promises belong to us—and which do not. For instance, God promised Abraham, not me and not you, that He would give Abraham offspring. We can't go around claiming that promise for ourselves.

We might like to think that every promise God made in the Bible is ours for the claiming. But they aren't. Some promises were made to specific people at specific times. Others are for all of God's people for all time. Sometimes we want to claim as a promise what is simply a general principle (most of the proverbs). Knowing the difference helps us know how to cling to God and His Word.

Here are some promises that do *not* belong to us because they were either made to a specific person at a specific time or because they are general principles not meant to be guaranteed promises:

> Arise, walk through the length and the breadth
> of the land, for I will give it to you.

GENESIS 13:17

> Train up a child in the way he should go; even
> when he is old he will not depart from it.

PROVERBS 22:6

> Jesus said to them, "Truly, I say to you, in the new world, when the
> Son of Man will sit on his glorious throne, you who have followed me
> will also sit on twelve thrones, judging the twelve tribes of Israel."

MATTHEW 19:28

Here are some promises that *do* belong to us:

> The steadfast love of the LORD never ceases; his mercies never come
> to an end; they are new every morning; great is your faithfulness.

LAMENTATIONS 3:22-23

> In my Father's house are many rooms. If it were not so,
> would I have told you that I go to prepare a place for you?
> And if I go and prepare a place for you, I will come again and
> will take you to myself, that where I am you may be also.

JOHN 14:2-3

And we know that for those who love God all things work together for good, for those who are called according to his purpose.

ROMANS 8:28

For I am sure that neither death nor life, nor angels nor rulers, nor things present nor things to come, nor powers, nor height nor depth, nor anything else in all creation, will be able to separate us from the love of God in Christ Jesus our Lord.

ROMANS 8:38-39

No temptation has overtaken you that is not common to man. God is faithful, and he will not let you be tempted beyond your ability, but with the temptation he will also provide the way of escape, that you may be able to endure it.

1 CORINTHIANS 10:13

I will never leave you nor forsake you.

HEBREWS 13:5b

If we confess our sins, he is faithful and just to forgive us our sins and to cleanse us from all unrighteousness.

1 JOHN 1:9

And I heard a loud voice from the throne saying, "Behold, the dwelling place of God is with man. He will dwell with them, and they will be his people, and God himself will be with them as their God. He will wipe away every tear from their eyes, and death shall be no more, neither shall there be mourning, nor crying, nor pain anymore, for the former things have passed away."

REVELATION 21:3-4

As Christians, we cling to God's Word. Knowing that God is able and faithful to keep His Word is not only comforting, but it's also central to our understanding of who God is. Numbers 23:19 says, "God is not human, that he should lie, not a human being, that he should change his mind. Does he speak and then not act? Does he promise and not fulfill?" (NIV). Our God is a promise-keeping God.

> How does this truth help you follow in the footsteps of Abraham's faith and "not waver in unbelief at God's promise but [be] strengthened in [your] faith and [give] glory to God, because [you are] fully convinced that what God [has] promised, he [is] also able to do" (Rom. 4:20-21, CSB)?

The promises of God are worth memorizing. We all face times when our circumstances appear hopeless. When those times come, place your hope in God and His Word. Know what He has promised. Believe He is able to keep His promises. Wait on His perfect timing. And grow strong in your faith as you cling to His Word.

> What is one thing you are currently hoping for, and where does your hope reside? How does our focus passage for today help you?

Abraham knew the promises of God. He believed them. Then after twenty-five years, he saw the glimmer of their fulfillment. Faith isn't believing that God will give us everything we want, in the way we want, when we want. Faith is believing that God will accomplish all of His purposes in His way, in His timing—all for our good and His glory.

> As you work on your memory verses, reflect on three to five mercies you have seen in the passages from Romans we've studied this session.

DIGGING DEEPER
Check out these verses to help you better understand today's passage:
2 Timothy 1:12 • 2 Timothy 3:14-17 • Hebrews 6:17-20

Session Four: THE GREATEST NEWS OF ALL TIME

WATCH Session Four video teaching.

1. But now

_____

_____

_____

_____

_____

_____

_____

2. In Christ

_____

_____

_____

_____

_____

_____

_____

_____

_____

DISCUSSION QUESTIONS

1   What day of personal study had the most impact on you? Why?

2   How did what you heard on the video teaching clarify, reinforce, or give new insight to what you studied this session?

3   What difference does it make that we are justified by God's grace as a gift and not because of our works?

4   Which is harder for you to believe—that your good works don't earn you any credit with God or that your bad works (sins) don't count against you? Explain.

5   What did you learn about faith this session? In what ways will those insights shape how you lean on the promises of God?

6   What new mercies did you see in the passage this session?

7   What is the most significant thing you learned about God, the gospel, or yourself this session?

To access the video teaching sessions, use the instructions in the back of your Bible study book.

SESSION FOUR   85

SESSION FIVE

Mercy Frees Us

ROMANS 5–7

Introduction

Have you ever seen one of those infomercials where the actor lists the many benefits of the product he's selling? Then, as he finishes extolling several virtues, he pauses and adds, "But wait. There's more!" In the course of the advertisement, he not only highlights the main product but all of the additional products that come with the main one.

In a much, much greater way, Romans 5–7 is Paul's, "But wait. There's more!" If the good news of our salvation stopped at the end of Romans 4, it would be more than enough. To know that God, the righteous Judge, has declared us—unrighteous, guilty, and condemned sinners—righteous, innocent, and not guilty is amazingly wonderful news. But Paul wanted us to know that's not all. The good news just keeps getting better and better. No matter how much you've tasted the goodness of the gospel, there's always more.

God's salvation results in the ever-overflowing mercy of God. In the same way a stone tossed into a lake produces ripples that spread out from the point of impact, so our great salvation produces many glorious results that ripple into our lives—peace, joy, hope, the love of God, freedom, and the ability to obey God's good Law.

Consider how the writer of the magnificent hymn, "Great Is Thy Faithfulness," captured this perfectly.

> Pardon for sin and a peace that endureth,
>
> thine own dear presence to cheer and to guide,
>
> strength for today and bright hope for tomorrow;
>
> blessings all mine, with ten thousand beside![1]

Peace, presence, strength, and hope. Mercies all mine, with ten thousand beside.

MEMORY VERSE

For the wages of sin is death, but the free gift of God is eternal life in Christ Jesus our Lord.

ROMANS 6:23

Prayer for the Week

Father, You are God alone—the Almighty, high and lifted up. You are the Holy One and worthy of my praise. Thank You for sending Jesus to save me. Thank You for loving me. Thank You for giving me a new heart and the gift of faith. As I study this week, open my eyes to see great and wondrous truths in Your Word. Change me, O God. Conform me more to the image of Your perfect Son and give me both the desire and the opportunity to tell others about Him. In His glorious name I pray, **Amen.**

DAY 1

THE GIFT OF PEACE

READ ROMANS 5:1-11.

In this passage, Paul transitioned from telling us what has happened (we've been justified by grace through faith) to explaining how that justification impacts our daily life. If you're like me, you want to know how the moments of your day are to be lived in light of the great truths we studied last session. We know our justification means we will be saved for all eternity, but does it change the way I live in the meantime? Paul said, *Absolutely!* The gospel doesn't just change our eternal future; it changes our present reality.

What Does It Say?

It will be helpful to pay attention to the verb tenses this session. Paul fluidly referred to past actions, current realities, and future events. Review verses 1–11 and then make a list of what you find under each heading.

Past Actions	Current Realities	Future Events

Write five benefits of our justification Paul listed in verses 1-5 and the four words he used to describe us in verses 6-10.

Five benefits of our justification (vv. 1–5):

VERSE 1	
VERSE 2	
VERSE 2	
VERSES 3-4	
VERSE 5	

Four words that describe us (vv. 6-10)

VERSE 6	
VERSE 6	
VERSE 8	
VERSE 10	

What three things do we rejoice (boast, glory) in (vv. 2,3,11)?

Rejoicing, or boasting, in suffering (v. 3) seems counterintuitive at best. When most people think about God's blessings, few consider the ability to rejoice in suffering as one. Yet it is one of the greatest benefits for a Christian. Suffering, trials, and hardship are common to everyone who has ever lived. The joy of salvation does not mean believers are spared from grief, sorrow, and pain—in fact, for many, faith in Jesus means increased suffering.

Our suffering is not meaningless, however. God promises not the absence of suffering but greater blessing through suffering. He uses hard things in our lives to accomplish greater things in us. He shows us more of Himself, strengthens us, and creates perseverance through suffering. He draws near and conforms us more to the image of Jesus, the Man of sorrows, through sorrow.

This doesn't mean the suffering Christian is supposed to "put on a happy face" or deny the reality or depth of pain being endured. But it does mean the distressed saint can cry out in honest faith, *Lord, I don't understand, but I trust that You love me and are working something good in me. I trust that my suffering is not in vain—and for that I praise You. I ask that You pour Your love into my heart through the Holy Spirit in real and tangible ways today.*

What Does It Mean?

> Paul listed peace with God as the first glorious result of our salvation. Why do you think Paul listed peace first? How is peace related to the reconciliation Paul wrote about in verses 10-11?

Notice that Paul did not say we have the peace of God. As lovely and available as that is to believers, in these verses, Paul said we have peace with God! The peace of God is delightful, but peace with God is astounding. We're all born as God's enemy—haters, rebels, and traitors. But God, being rich in mercy, ended the war, made peace, reconciled us, brought us close, and poured His love into our hearts. We didn't earn these things, deserve them, or accomplish them. God Himself accomplished and guarantees our eternal salvation, which means we can't reverse, negate, or lose it. If God has made peace with you through the blood of Jesus, then you're eternally safe in the arms of your Father.

> How would you describe the relationships between peace (v. 1), access (v. 2), joy (v. 3), endurance (v. 3), and hope (v. 4)? Why is this progression significant?

What Do I Do?

Have you ever explained salvation by saying, "Jesus died on the cross (past event) to take me to heaven (future event)"? It's true—but it's not all! Our salvation is past, present, and future. Jesus accomplished our salvation in the past when He lived, died, and rose again. In the future, at Christ's second coming, that glorious time when His eternal kingdom will be fully established, our salvation will be fully realized. But our salvation also impacts us now.

Using verses 1-11, how would you explain the gospel (past, present, and future) to someone who doesn't know Jesus? How would you explain the beautiful benefits of salvation in the day-to-day lives of believers?

What differences do each of the following make in your life today?	
Peace	
Access	
Joy	
Endurance	
Hope	

God has accomplished everything needed to save us. We can rest assured that our future salvation is guaranteed. As we wait for that glorious day, let's rejoice in the peace He's made, the access He's given, the endurance He cultivates, the hope He anchors, and the love He pours out.

DIGGING DEEPER
Check out these verses to help you better understand today's passage:
John 14:1-3 • 2 Corinthians 4:16-18 • Hebrews 10:19-22

DAY 2

THE GIFT OF RIGHTEOUSNESS

READ ROMANS 5:12-20.

Our passage today takes us back to the garden of Eden and the beginning of the story of our great redemption. Paul explained how the events of long-ago changed and impacted everything about our lives today. If you've ever wondered why the struggle against sin is so hard, why death is so grievous, or how the world came to be this way, Romans 5 tells us.

What Does It Say?

According to verses 12-20, answer the following questions:

How did sin come into the world, and what was the result (vv. 12,19)?

What is the free gift (v. 17)?

How was the gift obtained, and what is the result (vv. 15,18,19)?

Have you ever wondered what Adam's sin has to do with yours? Theologically speaking, it's one of the most important concepts we need to understand—the idea that one person stands as the representative of a larger group, and that what is true for the representative is true for the group.

Adam, as the first man, stood as the representative head of the entire human race. His actions affected not only himself, but every human born after him. His failure in the garden not only cast him into sin, death, and misery, but it did the same for every human being that followed him. All would be born as sinners under the curse of death.

The good news, however, is that Jesus also came as a representative head—the second Adam. Whereas all in Adam are condemned, all those in Christ are justified. Where Adam failed, Jesus succeeded. Where Adam was unrighteous and sinned, Jesus was perfectly righteous and sinless. As a result, when we repent of our sins and confess Christ as Savior and Lord, we're united to our new representative head and given all that His actions earned—life, justification, and righteousness. As one scholar said, "If in Adam, we are sinners; if in Christ, we are righteous."[2]

> What beautiful word (or two-word phrase, depending on your translation) is used five times in verses 15–17? How does verse 17 offer a definition for the word/phrase?

What Does It Mean?

> How would you explain the following phrases from verses 13 and 20?

> "sin indeed was in the world before the law was given" (v. 13):

> "but sin is not counted where there is no law" (v. 13):

> "the law came in to increase the trespass" (v. 20):

In order to understand what Paul was saying, we need two things: a little biblical-historical timeline and to know the difference between *sin* and *trespass*. Adam's sin is recorded in Genesis 3. But God didn't begin to give His Law through Moses until Exodus 20. Because we can read about the wickedness of humanity between Genesis 3 and Exodus 19, we know that Paul cannot mean that people were not sinful before the Law was given. He emphasized that fact by pointing out that "death [still] reigned" during that time (Rom. 5:14). And it wasn't that God didn't hold them accountable for their sin—just read about the flood in Genesis 6–9! Paul's point in verse 20 is that the Law was not given to provide life and righteousness; it only made us more aware of our sin.

Think of a child running wildly through the house, screaming, knocking things over, and jumping on furniture. Even if the parent never explicitly told the child not to do this, a child intuitively knows he or she shouldn't act like that. But if the parent told the child to stop, the culpability of the child only increases. The behavior was wrong prior to the "law;" the law only served to increase the trespass. The law didn't create the sin; it exposed the sin.

This leads us to the difference between sin and a trespass. **SIN** is loving or worshiping anything more than we love or worship God. It's spiritual idolatry, adultery, and treason. Or as my friend Dr. Jay Sklar said, "While sin is sometimes thought of today as the breaking of a rule, [the Bible] emphasizes that it is the breaking of a relationship," whereas a **TRESPASS** breaks an explicit command.[3] So you can see how "sin indeed was in the world before the law was given" (Rom. 5:13), but "the law came in to increase the trespass" (v. 20).

> In your own words, compare and contrast what Adam did with what Jesus did.

Similarities:

Differences:

> Using whatever creativity the Lord has given you (because He has given us varying degrees and abilities—me, less than most!), draw something (a chart, picture, graph . . .) that represents your answer above.

SIN
The New City Catechism defines sin as "rejecting or ignoring God in the world he created, rebelling against him by living without reference to him, not being or doing what he requires in his law—resulting in our death and the disintegration of all creation."[4]

TRESSPASS
Breaking an explicit command

What Do I Do?

What reigns over you? Our passage for today makes it clear that for everyone still in Adam, sin and death reign. But for all who are now in Christ, righteousness, grace, and life reign—abound even. Meaning, Jesus is greater, stronger, and more powerful than all our sin. He has provided the way for us to no longer live under the reign of sin but under the reign of grace.

In what ways do you live as though you are still in Adam, allowing sin to reign in your life?

The free gift of God is righteousness reigning in my life through Christ (v. 17). In the same way that I expect my children to open and use the gifts I give them, God doesn't want His gift to be left wrapped under some hypothetical tree. Receive His gift; delight in it; live in it!

In what ways do you live out the truth of who you are in Christ? How do you experience His grace and allow His righteousness to reign in your life?

As you work on your memory verse today, if you are in Christ, take time to praise Him for rescuing you from the domain of sin and death. If you still live under the reign of sin and death, the King of glory was sent to rescue and transfer you into the reign of grace and life. Run to Him.

DIGGING DEEPER
Check out these verses to help you better understand today's passage:
1 Corinthians 15:20-22 • 1 Corinthians 15:54-57 • Colossians 1:13-14

DAY 3

THE GIFT OF NEW LIFE

READ ROMANS 6:1-23.

I knew a man who professed belief in Christ, went to church, attended Bible studies—yet led one of the most blatantly immoral lives I've ever seen. His answer for the discrepancy between his professed faith and his lack of morality was, "I live in grace."

He completely misunderstood grace! Grace doesn't free us to sin; grace frees us from sin. There are two erroneous views of the doctrine of salvation by grace alone: one is polar opposite; the other is grievously distorted. The former we call *legalism*, which says stop sinning, do good things, and you will be saved. Paul had already argued vehemently that good works are not the root of our salvation but the fruit. The grievously distorted view is called *antinomianism*, which means to stop following the Law or any moral code and do what you want because you're under grace.[5] This falsehood is what the man in the example above believed. Paul confronted this lie head on in today's passage.

What Does It Say?

What questions did Paul imagine someone asking in verses 1 and 15?

What verse(s) in yesterday's passage might have prompted those questions?

What was Paul's answer to both questions?

It's so easy to read these verses and think God is telling us to die to sin. But He's not. He's telling us that if we're united to Christ, we have already died to sin! Most of these verses aren't commands to obey; they're truths to believe.

Fill in the following truth-statement blanks. If I am in Christ, then I . . .

Have been _____ into Christ (v. 3).

Was _____ with Christ (v. 4).

Have been _____ with Christ (v. 5).

Was _____ with Christ (v. 6).

Have _____ with Christ (v. 8).

Have been _____ from sin (v. 18).

We're not hoping for these statements to be true one day—they're true today for those in Christ. We're called to know what is true (vv. 3,6,9,16), believe that truth, and then walk in it.

Fill in the following blanks. Since I am in Christ, then I . . .

Can _____ in newness of life (v. 4).

Am able to consider myself _____ to _____ (v. 11).

Know that sin has no _____ over me (v. 14).

Have become a slave of _____ (v. 18).

What Does It Mean?

These verses don't mean we will achieve a perfectly sinless life. As one scholar said, "We cannot say, 'I will never sin again.' But we can say, 'I need not sin now. At this moment I am free not to sin.'"[6] We have been set free from the domain and reign of sin and need not obey its wicked rule any longer! Say it with me, "I need not sin now." That's the power of the cross. That's freedom.

What do you think, "having been set free from sin, [you] have become slaves of righteousness" means (v. 18)?

God doesn't just set us free from the dominion of sin to roam around aimlessly on our own. He brings us into His kingdom and His family. As a result, not only are we free to not sin, we're also free to pursue holiness and righteousness. In fact, we're obligated to! The freedom we're given allows us to pursue that which we were created for—holiness and righteousness.

Our Christian lives should reflect that reality more and more and more as time goes by. No one will be sinless in this life, but every true believer should see real change over time. In verses 19 and 22, Paul told us this ever-increasing fruit of righteousness is called **SANCTIFICATION**. Our sanctification begins the moment we're saved (justified) and doesn't end until we're in the eternal presence of Jesus (glorified).

SANCTIFICATION
The lifelong process of being increasingly conformed to Jesus' righteousness through the work of the Holy Spirit.

An important part of our sanctification is doing what Paul said in verse 11, "So you also must consider yourselves dead to sin and alive to God in Christ Jesus."

> **How might both parts of our current status (dead to sin and alive to Christ) help us pursue righteousness?**

What Do I Do?

Christopher Ash told the story "of a great eagle tethered to a post, walking sadly round and round. One day a new owner announced he would release the bird. A crowd gathered, the rope was removed—and the eagle continued walking round and round in the same old rut. He was free to fly and yet did not. The sad absurdity of that scene is like the Christian who continues in sin."[7]

The eagle, in order to be truly free, needed to first know he was free, then believe he was free, and, subsequently, fly. Each step is important—and ones we need to take, too. We need to know what our status is: dead to sin and alive to God in Christ. We need to believe this is true and then actively pursue this truth by walking in it. The question is not, *Did you believe God twenty years ago for your salvation?* The question is, *Are you believing Him today?* Do you tell yourself, *I'm just a sinner and therefore I can't help the sin I do?* Or do you tell yourself the truth, *I'm a redeemed sinner who has been set free and doesn't have to obey that cruel master anymore.*

> Is there a particular sin you feel has dominion over you? Explain. What truths from this passage empower you to walk away from that old master?

Let me say it again—no one will stop sinning completely in this life. (More about that on Day Five.) But in today's text, Paul wanted us to understand that the saved person has been set free not just from the penalty of sin, but from the power of sin. Because of that truth, we must fight to decrease the practice of sin.

> Take a few minutes and ask the Holy Spirit to show you where you might have used or are currently using the excuse "I live in grace" to sin. If He does, how do these verses challenge, convict, or help you?

Be encouraged; God is gracious. Our salvation begins with His grace; we are sanctified by His grace, and we will be glorified by His grace. Instead of using this glorious grace as an excuse to sin, live under its glorious reign and allow it to conform you to be more and more like the One to whom you're united.

DIGGING DEEPER
Check out these verses to help you better understand today's passage:
2 Corinthians 5:17 • Galatians 5:1 • 1 Peter 1:14-16

DAY 4

THE GIFT OF THE LAW

READ ROMANS 7:1-12.

When my oldest child began to crawl, I was shocked to see the first glimpse of his rebellious nature. He crawled past an electrical outlet he had played near numerous times. Trying to be proactively cautious, I walked over to the outlet, secured his attention, and stated clearly and loudly, "No touch." He turned, looked at me, and looked at the outlet. He then immediately crawled directly to it with an outstretched, chubby little hand, looked up at me, and touched the outlet. What had happened? Instead of producing right behavior, the law I laid down provoked in him the desire to rebel and disobey.

We're prone to respond similarly to God's Law. As one scholar said, "Sin is like fire, and the law is like oxygen. Oxygen is good, but it causes a fire to grow!"[8] The problem is not the Law. The problem is us and the sin in us.

What Does It Say?

What did Paul say about the Law in each of the following verses?

Verse 1	
Verse 4	
Verse 7	
Verse 10	
Verse 12	

It can be difficult at first glance to know if Paul thought the Law was bad (it arouses our sinful passions, brings sin to life, and proves to be death) or if the Law was good (see v. 12). The question, however, shouldn't be whether the Law is good or bad. (It's definitely good!) Instead, let's ask, *What is it that the Law can and cannot do?*

Historically, theologians talk about the three uses of the Law. The terms usually applied are:

CIVIL: Like a fence, the Law serves to restrain sinful behavior and promote righteous behavior (for example, don't steal, don't murder, honor your father and mother, and so forth). This use of the Law is meant to benefit and protect society at large.

PEDAGOGICAL: Like a mirror, the Law tells us what sin is and reveals that we are sinners. This use of the Law is meant to drive us to Jesus.

NORMATIVE: Like a lamp, the Law serves to illumine God's perfect, righteous character and instruct us on how to please Him. This use of the Law shows believers what life by the Spirit looks like.

What Does It Mean?

How are we to understand Paul's use of the marriage metaphor in verses 2-3? He was certainly not giving a definitive instruction on divorce and remarriage. Rather, he turned to this familiar cultural norm to say that in the same way a wife's obligation to the marriage ended when her husband died, we have died with Christ—we have been released from the unattainable demands of the Law. Dr. Dan Doriani explained it like this:

> Until Christ came, humanity was bound to the law, which Paul compares to a husband from whom liberation might be desirable. If that husband dies, obligations to him cease (7:1-3). In 7:4, Paul alters the metaphor and says "you have died to the law." . . . Specifically, since Jesus kept the law and bore the price of disobedience to it in his body, we are not liable to punishment and condemnation for failing to keep the law. So we are "released from the law" as someone might be released from a destructive marriage.[9]

According to verse 4, for what purpose have we been released from the demands of the Law? How is this in contrast with the fruit mentioned in verse 5?

How would you explain to a new Christian that we have been released from the Law's demands but the Law is still good?

The Law is good. We just can't ask it to do what it wasn't designed to do. It can reveal sin, but it can't heal us from sin. The Law can show us our need for a Savior, but it can't save us. And obedience to the Law isn't what sanctifies us. The Spirit does.

RESOURCE RECOMMENDATION
Ten Words to Live By
by Jen Wilkin

In what ways can you relate to Paul's story about himself in verses 7–8? Which of the uses of the Law listed on page 102 do you think he was referring to?

Paul focused in on the tenth commandment, "You shall not covet" (v. 7). The New City Catechism tells us this commandment requires "that we are content, not envying anyone or resenting what God has given them or us."[10] Contentment is hard for all of us. We look around and covet possessions, gifts, abilities, opportunities, beauty, husbands, marriages, children, parents, houses, vacations, platforms, careers, success, lifestyles . . . truly to infinity. As my friend Melissa Kruger said, "Coveting does not result because we don't have something. We covet because we fail to believe something."[11] We fail to believe that God and His ways are good. Coveting is a heart attitude gone awry that conveys a lack of trust and satisfaction in what the Lord has chosen both to give and to withhold.

In what ways is covetousness the root of all other sin? List three to five things you're currently tempted to covet.

What Do I Do?

I loved my mother-in-law. She was a bit of a pistol who, like my oldest child in the previous example, did not like to be told what to do or not do. Self-admittedly, she said the restraint itself made her want to do the forbidden activity even more. Her first response to being told she couldn't do something was inevitably, "Oh yeah? Watch me!" I can relate. A "KEEP OUT" sign on a door increases my desire to go into that room. A "Confidential: Do Not Open" stamp on the outside of an envelope makes me want to open and look inside. As Paul said, the sin (already in me) comes alive when the commandment is given.

In what ways does hearing the law stir up your desire to disobey that law?

Using the truths of our passage today, what would you say to someone who thinks she will go to heaven because she believes she hasn't broken any of the Ten Commandments? What would you say to someone who thinks she'll never go to heaven because she's broken one or more?

The Law is good because it shows us both the beauty of who God is by showing us His character while, at the same time, revealing our need for Jesus. When we are united to Jesus in faith, His perfect obedience to the Law is attributed to us. We are set free from the curse of the Law and, at the same time, made able to pursue the beauty of the Law in joy, gratitude, and love of the One who saved us.

As you work on your memory verse today, thank God for His good Law and for fulfilling it on our behalf.

DIGGING DEEPER
Check out these verses to help you better understand today's passage:
2 Corinthians 3:4-6 • Galatians 2:19-21 • Colossians 2:13-14

DAY 5

THE GIFT OF THE STRUGGLE

READ ROMANS 7:13-25.

All session we've been glorying in the truths of our victory and freedom in Christ. Did you, like me, on Day Two, feel the joy of righteousness reigning in life through Jesus? Or, on Day Three, triumphantly say, "I need not sin now—I have died to sin." Or, on Day Four, rest in the fact that you've been released from the captivity of the Law? It's been a week full of deep, profound, and life-altering truths.

But on any of those days, did you, like me, close your Bible and within twenty-or-so minutes of glorying in the remarkable truths of your freedom from sin, proceed to sin in some way? Ugh. Don't you hate that? Have you ever wondered why, if you and I are dead to sin, it seems to rear its ugly head in our lives so often? If so, then we're going to be greatly encouraged by Paul's words for us today. Not in the "misery loves company" kind of way, but in the "I'm not alone" kind of way.

There is debate over exactly who Paul was referring to in these verses. Was Paul describing himself struggling with sin before he became a Christian or after he became one? I'm persuaded (and comforted!) that Paul is talking about his life after he became a Christian.

Regardless of where you land in the debate, the truth we all can agree on is that real Christians really struggle with real sin. And, as we'll see, the struggle itself is evidence of new life.

We're going to depart from our normal format today (*What does it say? What does it mean? What do I do?*), and instead ask a series of questions to better understand Paul's main point.

RESOURCE RECOMMENDATIONS

To better understand the argument, the following three articles, which you can find on thegospelcoalition.org, clearly explain three differing views:

"Romans 7 Does Describe Your Christian Experience," by John Piper

"Romans 7 Does Not Describe Your Christian Experience," by Thomas Schreiner

"Lloyd-Jones: Believer or Unbeliever Is Not the Point of Romans 7," by Ben Bailie

What did Paul say produced death in him (v. 13)? What did Paul continue to say is good?

Paul stated that he loved God's Law and hated his own sin. Unbelievers don't say that! Only someone who has been regenerated by the Holy Spirit can say they love God's Law and hate their sin. Before I was a Christian, I thought the sins I committed were funny and fun at best and trivial and inconsequential at worst. Basically, I enjoyed sinning and didn't try not to. I thought God's Law was irrelevant, outdated, and downright silly for the most part.

As a believer, however, I hate my sin (not as much as I should, but more and more each day), and I love God's Word. I desperately want it to convict, rebuke, and instruct me. Here's the point: the love of God's Word and the struggle against sin testifies that we belong to God. The struggle itself is a sign of new life.

For each of the following verses, give an example from your own life of a time you experienced what Paul was describing:

"For I do not understand my own actions. For I do not do what I want, but I do the very thing I hate" (v. 15).

"For I have the desire to do what is right, but not the ability to carry it out" (v. 18b).

"For I do not do the good I want, but the evil I do not want is what I keep on doing" (v. 19).

Nobody's path of sanctification is a straight line from A to B.

For most of us, it looks more like this.

When we accept Christ, our justification is instantaneous. God declares us not guilty and we are immediately justified. Our glorification will be instantaneous, too. In 1 Corinthians 15:52, Paul wrote, "in the twinkling of an eye, at the last trumpet . . . the dead will be raised imperishable, and we shall be changed." But our sanctification is progressive, slow at times, faster at others. We hit bumps and stumble around a bit, but, overall, we're continually being transformed "from one degree of glory to another" (2 Cor. 3:18).

> Name one area in your life where you see sanctification occurring. (Think about an area of your life where you used to struggle with sin but now see victory and more conformity to Jesus). Stop and praise God for it!

After studying Romans 6, you might be confused. Are we dead to sin or not? Can we say, "I need not sin now" or not? Yes and yes. The battle has been definitively won. Jesus conquered sin and sin's heinous consequence, death. If you are in Christ, the victory is yours. Today. But our old enemy still calls our name. We still listen. And sometimes we fight the sin he tempts us with more than at other times. As John Piper said, "the victory [which has been accomplished] does not make the warfare [the struggle] past; it makes it possible and real."[12] When we fight against sin, we fight as those to whom the victory has already been given.

When is the last time you, like Paul, wanted to do right but found evil close at hand (Rom. 7:21)?

The patterns of the old life are hard to unlearn. Imagine moving to a different country. You would have to work to learn the customs of your new home. But the ways of your old country would still be with you. You wouldn't unlearn them. In fact, your tendency might be to revert to your old customs even though you're living in a new land. Sometimes the old customs might seem easier than the new ones. Sometimes you might simply forget the new ways. Or sometimes you might actually prefer your old ways.

Of course, cultures and customs are not wrong or sinful (just the opposite—they're to be celebrated!), but our battle to leave sin behind is similar—when we are united to Christ, we leave our old country of sin behind. But it's hard to unlearn everything that was a custom or habit to us in our old land. Sometimes it's hard for us to remember the new ways. And, sadly, sometimes, we simply long for and prefer our old ways.

What did Paul cry out in verse 24? Have you ever felt the same anguish? Explain.

The bad news is that, in some ways, the struggle only intensifies as we mature in the Lord. The longer I walk with God, the more I know Him, the greater my love grows for Him, and the more I recognize and despise my sin. Not just the outward, obvious ones, but also the more subtle and more "acceptable" sins like bitterness, refusal to forgive, selfish decisions, love of money, fear of the future, desire for approval, and so forth. Plus, the Lord continues to show me that sin is so deeply entwined in me that sometimes even the good I do is coupled with impure motives and tainted with sin. Like Paul, I cry out, *Who will deliver me from this body of death?*

Where did Paul turn for deliverance (v. 25)?

The Law can't save us; only Jesus can. Paul cried out to Jesus in confidence and hope. Jesus was the One who delivered him from his body of death and his struggle with sin. Oh sister, are you struggling, stumbling, or feeling defeated? Are you trying to battle in your own strength? You can't overcome in your own strength. Cry out to Jesus.

If you are feeling overwhelmed, defeated, or discouraged by your sin, I want you to do something we don't normally do.

> **Look ahead in your Bible to the very next verse, Romans 8:1, and write it here.**

The enemy of your soul would love to see you return to his bondage. But you've been set free. And he would love to convince you that your present struggle with sin condemns you. But thanks be to God in Jesus Christ our Lord—it doesn't! In fact, as we stated earlier, the struggle itself testifies that you belong to Jesus.

Let me leave you with two Scripture verses to meditate on and use in the midst of your struggle.

> No temptation has overtaken you that is not common to man. God is faithful, and he will not let you be tempted beyond your ability, but with the temptation he will also provide the way of escape, that you may be able to endure it.

1 CORINTHIANS 10:13

> And I am sure of this, that he who began a good work in you will bring it to completion at the day of Jesus Christ.

PHILIPPIANS 1:6

Name three to five mercies you have seen in our passages this session.

DIGGING DEEPER
Check out these verses to help you better understand today's passage:
Psalm 1:1–3 • 2 Corinthians 3:18 • Galatians 5:16–24

Session Five: DEAD TO SIN

WATCH Session Five video teaching.

1. New creation

Creation	Fall/Rebellion	Redemption	New Creation
_____ to sin	Not _____ to _____ sin	_____ to _____ sin	Not _____ to sin

_____

_____

_____

_____

_____

2. New struggle

_____

_____

_____

_____

_____

_____

_____

_____

_____

_____

DISCUSSION QUESTIONS

1   What day of personal study had the most impact on you? Why?

2   How did what you heard on the video teaching clarify, reinforce, or give new insight to what you studied this session?

3   In Romans 5:1, Paul listed peace with God as the first glorious result of our salvation. Why do you think that is so important? How is peace related to the reconciliation Paul wrote about in Romans 5:10-11?

4   Are there areas in your life where you see evidence that you are living as though you're still in Adam? Where can you see the fruit of knowing you're in Christ?

5   How does knowing you are both dead to sin and alive to Christ (Rom. 6:11) help you pursue righteousness?

6   What new mercies did you see in the passage this session?

7   What is the most significant thing you learned about God, the gospel, or yourself this session?

To access the video teaching sessions, use the instructions in the back of your Bible study book.

Mercy Holds Us

ROMANS 8

Introduction

Nobody would accuse me of being a great or serious hiker. I'm more of a sidewalk stroller than a mountain climber. But I have hiked a little. The hardest hike I ever completed was up the side of a mountain called Twin Sisters in the Colorado Rockies outside Estes Park. In addition to a challenging trail, this particular hike had an insane departure time of 4 a.m.

I was serving as a counselor for the youngest campers at a camp dedicated to kids with burn injuries. One little girl in my cabin stood out. At seven years old, she was the youngest camper we had. Her injuries had left her without toes, with misshapen feet, and the need for crutches. Yet she had no intention of missing out on this challenging and brutally early hike. So I promised her we would hike together.

The trail was steep. We stopped frequently for sips of water and bites of an energy bar, but we continued to trudge up the mountain. It was hard. There were times I carried my little friend on my back. Despite the respite stops, we both struggled. But we made it. Just in time.

As we breathlessly joined the other camper-hikers already at the summit, we sat down and looked up. The reason for the unreasonably early departure quickly became clear. We were on the summit just as the sun began to rise over the Rocky Mountains. As the two of us sat side by side, slowly the light and warmth of the sun spread over the scene from east to west. It was arguably one of the most beautiful sights I have ever seen.

I'm far from the first to compare Romans 8 to the spectacular summit of a glorious mountain. John Stott compared Romans 1–7 as a "long uphill climb" where we are given brief respites (glimpses of God's grace, faithfulness, peace, joy, and hope).[1] These brief respites are like breaks in the foliage where we get short glimpses of good news along the long and arduous hike.

But turning the page to Romans 8 is like reaching the summit. We look up and see the panoramic view of God's majestic love—vast, splendid, and by far the most beautiful sight we will ever behold. The Son and the Spirit shine brighter and more radiantly than any mere sunrise. Come, sit with me on the summit and let's drink in the vista together.

MEMORY VERSES

> For I am sure that neither death nor life, nor angels nor rulers, nor things present nor things to come, nor powers, nor height nor depth, nor anything else in all creation, will be able to separate us from the love of God in Christ Jesus our Lord.

ROMANS 8:38-39

Prayer for the Week

Father, Son, and Holy Spirit, I bow before You

as I open Your Word. Would You meet with me

as I study this week? Remind and assure me of

Your great love. Comfort and strengthen me with

Your presence. Help me to believe these great

truths, endure any trial, delight in Your mighty

love, walk in Your Spirit, and rest in the power

of Your Son. In whose name I pray, **Amen.**

DAY 1

CURRENT FREEDOM

READ ROMANS 8:1-11.

We serve a triune God—one God who eternally exists in three Persons: Father, Son, and Spirit. All three members of the Trinity participated in the creation of all things, and all three members of the Trinity participate in making us new creations through salvation.

Most of us think predominantly about Jesus when we think about our salvation (i.e. Jesus died to save me from my sins). But salvation involves all three members of the Trinity. God the Father planned our salvation; God the Son accomplished our salvation, and God the Spirit applies our salvation. Their work is distinct but inseparable. Meaning, you don't receive the accomplishment of the Son without also receiving the indwelling of the Spirit.

What Does It Say?

Use the following chart to list where each member of the Trinity is mentioned in these verses and what we learn about each One. (Hint: when Paul said "God," he's usually talking about the Father even though all three members are fully God.)

	Where is He mentioned?	What do we learn?
Father		
Son		
Spirit		

THE FLESH
Here, this refers to everything in us that is fallen and sinful—everything that demands self-gratification and is opposed to the ways of God.

We're going to learn a lot more this session about the work of the Holy Spirit in our lives. One of the first great benefits of having the Holy Spirit living in us (v. 9) is that He shows us God's ways and helps us walk in them.

Paul drew sharp distinctions between life in **THE FLESH** and life in the Spirit. What distinctions did he make?

Life in the Flesh	Life in the Spirit

At the end of Romans 7, we empathized with Paul in his struggle against sin. Followers of Jesus find both encouragement and discouragement in that passage. We're encouraged by knowing we're not alone in our struggle with and hatred of besetting sins. But we're discouraged because we understand that those of us who love Jesus will increasingly hate our own sin. We long to be set free of the sin that so easily entangles.

Paul reminded us that we can! It's one of the reasons why Romans 8:1-11 is so encouraging. We see what having the Spirit of God dwelling in us looks like and how to walk accordingly. Unbelievers can only walk according to the flesh. Believers, because of the indwelling Holy Spirit, have a choice. We can choose to walk (or live our lives) according to the Spirit.

What Does It Mean?

The late Dr. R. C. Sproul said that Romans 8:1 is the gospel in a nutshell.[2]

What do you think *therefore* refers to? (Hint: flip back through your definitions and remind yourself what the opposite of justification is.)

What do you think each of the following words from verse 1 means?

Now	
No	
Condemnation	

What is the direct implication for your life?

To whom do the glorious truths of verse 1 apply?

But now! I am so grateful that we live in the time of *but now*. Now, there is no condemnation for anyone who is in Christ. Now, the saving work of Jesus is available to us through the ongoing work of the Spirit. Now, after salvation, the Spirit of God dwells in the children of God, teaching, rebuking, encouraging, directing, and helping us. Now, the Holy Spirit not only gives us new life (by uniting us to Jesus), He also shows us how to live the new life He has given.

What does it mean to set your mind on the things of the flesh and to set your mind on the things of the Spirit? How are these mindsets different?

Growing up, my mom had a little newspaper clipping taped to the wall by the phone. It read,

Little people talk about other people.

Average people talk about things.

Great people talk about ideas.

Since I spent a lot of time on the phone during my growing up years, my eyes probably drifted over this little piece of paper multiple times a day for over a decade. I have reflected back on that saying over the years and have concluded that, while there is some truth in it, verses 5-8 in our passage contain deeper truth. What we talk about is only a reflection of what we set our minds and center our lives on.

The focus of your life will determine the trajectory of your life. What you set your mind on will inform not only your speech, but also your thoughts, your decisions, and your actions. Setting your mind on the things of God means that you think about God, His Word, and His ways. You consider how those things inform and affect your life. You speak to others about these things. You seek the things of God, trust the ways of God, and live under the influence and authority of the Word of God.

For a quick diagnostic, pay attention to what you talk about with your friends and family. If most of your speech centers on the things this life offers—accomplishments, possessions, money, beauty—then chances are you have set your mind on the things of the flesh. The good news is that, if the Spirit of God lives in you, you are now able to set your mind on the things of God. As you do, you will see a change not only in what you talk about, but also in how you live, think, and act.

What Do I Do?

> What are some practical ways you can walk more and more in the Spirit who dwells in you? How does having your mind set on the Spirit offer life and peace to you (v. 6)?

Paul ended this section with an amazing statement. Go back and read verse 11.

> Do you believe that Jesus was really raised from the dead? If so, what true assurance does verse 11 offer you?

Paul said that if we are born again, then the Spirit who lives in us is the same Spirit that caused Jesus, crucified and dead, to rise from the grave. That same Spirit will one day raise your mortal body from the dead to live for all eternity. That is astounding hope! Do you believe it?

We all have moments of doubt. Fear of death is normal. Anxiety about the unknown can plague anyone. But God offers us real truth in His Word and that truth is meant to produce genuine hope and solid confidence in our moments of fear and doubt. This session we're going to see multiple truths laid out that are given for our assurance. Focus on them. Think about them. Believe them. And cling to them.

DIGGING DEEPER
Check out these verses to help you better understand today's passage:
Acts 13:38–39 • 1 Corinthians 6:19-20 • Colossians 3:1-4

DAY 2

PAST ADOPTION

READ ROMANS 8:12-17.

Our friends' oldest son befriended a classmate from a dysfunctional and abusive home. This classmate, let's call him Drew, began to spend more and more time with our friends' family. He ate meals with them, studied at their house, even joined them on family vacations. Eventually, out of necessity, he cut ties with his family of origin and moved into an upstairs bedroom at our friends' house.

This arrangement was working, but my friend and her husband wanted more than for Drew to live as a guest upstairs. They asked Drew if he wanted to be legally adopted by them. He did, and he was. As a legal son, he now has all the rights and responsibilities of their biological children. He assumed their last name—and will pass that name on to his own children one day. He is an heir and has an inheritance. Adoption sealed his place in the family—fully and permanently belonging.

Oh friend, how much more does our adoption into God's family mean to us! Many of us are so prone to the fear that we don't really belong to God, that maybe He's just letting us live "in the upstairs bedroom"—an arrangement that could end at any time. We long to know the surety and safety of our Father's permanent love. This assurance is just one of the beautiful ramifications of our adoption!

What Does It Say?

In verse 15, what are the two contrasting options? Describe the results of each.

What does the Spirit do in each of the following verses?

Verse 13:

Verse 14:

Verse 15:

Verse 16:

Adoption was a common practice for the Gentiles in first-century Rome where "childless couples adopted virtuous young men, faithful friends, and servants. The goal was to pass on the family name, land, and wealth to young and worthy adult men who would honor the family name."[3] In other words, adoption was more contractual than relational, more for the deserving than the helpless.

Our adoption is so different and so much more. As a classic Christian confession of faith so beautifully states:

> Those adopted enjoy the liberties and privileges of God's children, have his name put on them, receive the Spirit of adoption, have access to the throne of grace with boldness, and are enabled to cry, Abba, Father. They are pitied, protected, provided for, and disciplined by him as a father. They are never cast off, however, and are sealed until the day of redemption and inherit the promises as heirs of everlasting salvation.[4]

What Does It Mean?

The good news just keeps getting better and better, doesn't it? If you are in Christ, not only have you been declared not guilty, been declared righteous, been set free from slavery and sin, been given peace with God, hope in suffering, and access to Him—you have been adopted by the God of the universe. You are loved. Eternally. You will never be cast out. You will never be unloved. You will always be safe.

How does being adopted by God change the nature of our relationship with Him? How does it change the way you approach God?

It seems the two things that most easily cause us to fear when we've been separated from God and His love are sin and suffering. Our sin can cause us to fear that God wants nothing to do with us. Our suffering can cause us to fear that God doesn't really care. God, in His mercy, has already gone out of His way to assure us that our sin does not cause Him to pull away. We've read:

> God's love has been poured into our hearts through the Holy Spirit who has been given to us.

ROMANS 5:5b

> . . . but God shows his love for us in that while we were still sinners, Christ died for us.

ROMANS 5:8

> There is therefore now no condemnation for those who are in Christ Jesus.

ROMANS 8:1

And in today's passage, God begins to assure us that suffering in no way means He has pulled back. In fact, in our suffering, He draws near.

List four to five things you learn about suffering in verse 17.

We are united to a Savior who suffered. When we are united to Christ, like we saw in the video for Session Four, we share in everything that is His—including His suffering. But we don't suffer alone. We suffer with Him. He suffers with us! Our suffering is not an indication that God has turned away. We are dearly loved children. Meaning, when suffering comes, and it will, we can run to our Father and cry to our **ABBA**. He will hold us close.

ABBA
The Aramaic word for *father* conveying affection, trust, and love. It is the term Jesus used as He prayed in the garden the night before He was crucified (Mark 14:36).

What Do I Do?

In what ways do you long to feel safe in the love of God? How do these verses assure you?

In what ways has the Spirit of God testified, or born witness, with your spirit that you are a child of God?

Go back and read the quote from the confession of faith on page 121. Of all the benefits and blessings of our adoption that are listed, pick one and write down how you can respond to that truth this week.

God is a perfect Father. He provides, protects, and pursues. His love is pure, perfect, and constant. He is trustworthy and good. As you work on your memory verse this week, my prayer is that the Spirit will testify with your soul that you are God's child—completely safe and eternally loved.

DIGGING DEEPER
Check out these verses to help you better understand today's passage:
Hosea 1:10 • John 1:12-13 • Ephesians 5:1-2

PRESENT SUFFERINGS

READ ROMANS 8:18-25.

People who run marathons say the sense of accomplishment at the finish line is worth the pain experienced in the race. People who undergo hard surgeries and long recoveries say it's worth it to be free of the illness and pain they had before the surgery. Women who endure difficult deliveries say the joy of the baby is worth the pain of labor. We endure all sorts of hard things because something greater is on the other side.

Even so, Paul's claim in verse 18 is astounding.

What Does It Say?

What did Paul say about our sufferings in verse 18?

No comparison. Not even in the same ballpark. The glory so completely outweighs the suffering that you can't even call it a comparison. How could Paul say that? Did he not know human suffering? Did he not understand the grief, the tears, the heartache, the agony, the disappointment, the loneliness, and the pain we face? Some of us have been through unimaginable loss. Some of us live with unspeakable pain. Was Paul saying these are insignificant things?

Not at all. Paul knew suffering. (See 2 Cor. 11:24-28.) He knew the weight and the depth of grief. What he said is that the glory awaiting us is unfathomably greater, deeper, weightier, and more, well, more glorious, than anything we can imagine. This wasn't just wishful thinking on Paul's part. This is God's promise to us. Suffering is horrible. Glory is incomparably greater.

The anticipation and surety of that glory informs how we are to live in the here-and-now. We, with all of creation, are to wait.

What is creation waiting for? How is it waiting?

What are we waiting for? How are we waiting?

What Does It Mean?

The word *glory* is used twice in this passage (vv. 18,21). What do you learn about glory in each verse?

Glory is hard to define because no one has fully seen it to be able to explain it. Oh, we get glimpses of glory's shadow now and then in creation and in God's Word—even Moses, who asked to see God's glory, saw only the back of it—yet Moses' face shone from that small glimpse (Ex. 33:18-23; 34:29-33). But no one has gazed unhindered on God's glory. It is going to be awesome. Literally. And one thing we learn in Romans 8 is that it "is not just that we will see *his* glory; it is that his glory will be seen in *us*."[5]

Why do you think Paul said "as we wait eagerly for adoption as sons" in verse 23 when he told us in yesterday's passage that we have already received the Spirit of adoption (v. 15) and already are God's children (v. 16)?

We live in the time of the "already and not yet." Jesus has already come; His kingdom has already been inaugurated, and we have already been saved. But Jesus has not yet come again; His kingdom has not yet been consummated, and we are not yet living with Him in glory. We have already been adopted but are not yet fully home.

What Do I Do?

What about the "not yet" do you most long for?

Verse 23 tells us that we, like all creation, "groan inwardly as we wait." A groan is a sound we make when words don't suffice—when we're wounded, burdened, or in despair. Naturally, in this world, we groan. But the amazing thing we'll see in tomorrow's passage is that the Spirit groans with us. He is with us in our suffering. He is with us in our tears. And He is with us as we wait for the indescribable glory that is coming.

Paul compared our groanings to the pains of childbirth. In what ways is that a helpful analogy?

What hope do these verses offer you in times of suffering?
Be as specific as possible.

We live in the days of suffering and groaning. But these days won't last forever. The day of glory is coming. And that day will be greater, brighter, happier, better, and lovelier than anything we can imagine now. So, as we wait, we hope; we cling, and we endure because we know that something far greater is on the other side.

DIGGING DEEPER
Check out these verses to help you better understand today's passage:
Isaiah 25:8-9 • 2 Corinthians 11:24-28 • Revelation 21:1-7

DAY 4

CONSTANT INTERCESSION

READ ROMANS 8:26-30.

We all yearn for assurance. We want to know that everything is going to be all right in the end. Young brides long for assurance that their marriages will go the distance. Cancer patients crave some guarantee they will be healed. People nearing retirement desire confidence that their savings will last their lifetimes. Mothers of young children pursue parenting formulas that will ensure their children "turn out OK." However, true guarantees are hard to come by.

But God goes out of His way to assure those of us who follow Christ that everything will be OK—infinitely better than "OK"—in the end. In this session alone we've read that we're guaranteed:

ETERNAL LIFE: "If the Spirit of him who raised Jesus from the dead dwells in you, he who raised Christ Jesus from the dead will also give life to your mortal bodies through his Spirit who dwells in you" (v. 11).

FOREVER ADOPTION: "For you did not receive the spirit of slavery to fall back into fear, but you have received the Spirit of adoption as sons, by whom we cry, 'Abba! Father!'" (v. 15).

A BEAUTIFUL INHERITANCE: ". . . and if children, then heirs—heirs of God and fellow heirs with Christ . . ." (v. 17a).

UNIMAGINABLE GLORY: "For I consider that the sufferings of this present time are not worth comparing with the glory that is to be revealed to us" (v. 18).

But as we sit on the summit here in Romans 8, viewing the vista of God's indescribable mercies, we just keep seeing more.

What Does It Say?

What "guarantees" do you see in the following verses?

Verses 26–27:

Verses 28–29:

Verse 30:

Romans 8:28 is one of the most comforting verses in all of Scripture. It has also been misused, misapplied, and mistimed. It's misused and misapplied when we imply it means that all things work together to give me exactly what I want or take it to mean nothing difficult or tragic will ever happen to me. And it's often mistimed when we offer it to others in the midst of fresh grief.

Well-intentioned people often stand at a distance and toss this verse out like a lifejacket to someone drowning in sorrow. That is usually not the time or place to offer this truth to others. Romans 8:28 is a truth we bury deep in our souls so that it will be a lifesaving truth we cling to in the midst of our own doubts and sorrows.

To whom does this promise in verse 28 apply?

Do we think, hope, or know this is true? What's the difference?

Which things work together? What does that mean?

What Does It Mean?

We don't always understand why God allows us to go through the difficulties we go through. We don't always know what He is doing or why. We can't fathom how situations are going to work out. But those aren't the things He promises us we'll know. What He has promised is that we can know (i.e. believe, trust, bank on, grasp . . .). He is at work for our good in the midst of everything we go through.

What do you think "good" in this verse means? How does verse 29 help us understand the meaning of "good"?

The reason God can make such a glorious promise to us is because He has a plan to save a people for Himself and He is sovereignly ruling over each and every step of that plan until it is fully realized. Paul used five words to explain the big picture of God's guarantee that He is working in all things to accomplish His magnificent plan of redemption.

What do you think each of the following words means?

Foreknew:

Predestined:

Called:

Justified:

Glorified:

CALLED
God's call is His summons to follow Him in much the same way Jesus called each of the disciples to follow Him.

GLORIFIED
To be glorified will be the final step in our salvation. It refers to when we will be with Jesus and be like Jesus. At that time, we will be free from the presence of sin (not able to sin!) and live fully in the presence of God.

Good scholars debate over the terms used in these two verses. Much of the discussion revolves around the word *foreknew*. Predestination (or election) refers to the "gracious purpose of God, according to which He regenerates, justifies, sanctifies, and glorifies sinners."[6] One of the main points of discussion however is the question of whether God's predestination is based on His foreknowledge of how a person will respond to His call for salvation or if His predestination is based on foreknowledge of His own sovereign mercy and will. Here are the two major interpretations in very simplified terms:

1. Some scholars believe *foreknew* means God looked through the corridors of time and saw how each person would respond to the gospel. Knowing who would accept God's gift of salvation, God predestined, or elected, them for salvation. In this view, God's call is based on His knowing ahead of time how that particular individual would respond—either by being obedient and following or by being rebellious and walking away.

2. Other scholars believe *foreknew* means that long before someone knows God, God set His love on that person and, as a result, predestined and elected that person to respond to His call. In other words, every individual whom God calls He enables to respond obediently by following Him.

My understanding aligns more closely with the second interpretation, but, regardless of your understanding, we can agree on the fact that "God has done all that is needed to secure our eternal glory,"[7] that everyone God saves will be conformed to the image of Jesus, and "*all* those with whom God begins this process complete it."[8] That is our deep assurance.

What Do I Do?

When was the last time you did "not know what to pray for as [you] ought" (v. 26)?

In what ways are each of the following promises comforting to you and helpful for your prayer life?

INTERCEDE
To pray, petition, and plead for another.

"The Spirit helps us in our weakness . . . [and] **INTERCEDES** with groanings too deep for words" (v. 26).

"The Spirit intercedes for the saints according to the will of God" (v. 27).

What comfort does verse 28 offer you today? How does it strengthen you?

What comfort do verses 29-30 offer you today? How do they strengthen you?

As you work on your memory verse today, thank God that He was at work in your past circumstances, is at work in your current situation, and will be at work in your future happenings, too. Thank Him that, through it all, He is working for your good, conforming you to Jesus. Thank Him that the Spirit is (and has been) constantly praying for you, helping you in your weakness. And thank Him that He will hold you fast and see you home to glory.

DIGGING DEEPER
Check out these verses to help you better understand today's passage:
John 6:39 • Ephesians 1:3-6 • 2 Timothy 1:8-9

DAY 5

NEVER SEPARATED

READ ROMANS 8:31-39.

Do you remember last session when we said that Romans 5–7 is Paul's, "But wait. There's more!"? Well, Romans 8:31-39 is the grand and glorious conclusion to all he has told us.

Paul wanted the reader to ponder the logical conclusion to all the truths he had shared.

Since . . .

- you have peace with God,

- you have access to the Father,

- you have hope in suffering,

- you've been set free from sin and death,

- you've been united to Christ,

- there's no condemnation.

What then shall we say to these things?

Picture Paul taking a deep, satisfied, joyful breath as he began to answer his own question . . . *Oh, let me tell you!*

If we've been sitting on the summit overlooking God's mercies this week as if they are the sun rising—getting brighter and brighter and more glorious and more glorious—then today is the day the sun fully breaks out over the entire mountain range. As you read the verses we're going to study today, you might feel like singing, dancing, and praising. Go ahead. I'll join you.

What Does It Say?

What questions did Paul ask in the following verses? (If Paul offered an answer, include that, too.)

Verse 31b:

Verse 33:

Verse 34:

The answer is always Jesus! Because Jesus was not spared, because Jesus died and was raised, because the Father gave us Jesus, we are guaranteed that no one can come against us or condemn us. No one! One commentator wrote, "When the accuser brings charges against Christians, he has to put a hand over his mouth when he sees the cross."[9] The sacrifice of Jesus guarantees our eternal place of safety before the Father.

Not only can no one condemn us; nothing can separate us, either. The cross of Christ doesn't just mean we're free; it means we are deeply loved and securely held.

Write the types of trials listed in verse 35 on the left side of the chart below.

In verses 38-39, Paul listed six things that cannot separate us from the love of God in Jesus (four are pairs and two are single). List them on the left side of the chart below.

What Does It Mean?

Go back to the two previous charts and, in the right column, put into your own words what each word or phrase on the left might mean.

Read verse 32 out loud five times. (Yes, really!) Let the truth sink deep into your soul. Scholars say that Paul is arguing from the greater thing (He's given us His Son!) to the lesser thing (how will He not also give us all things?).[10] It doesn't mean God will give us everything we want. It means He will give us everything we need. Everything.

Is there anything you feel God has withheld from you? What do you think Paul meant when he wrote "give us all things" (v. 32)?

How has God given you everything you need to walk through the trials and difficulties you listed in the charts?

What Do I Do?

In verse 37, Paul used a word he might have made up—ὑπερνικάω *(hypernikaō)*.[11] It means *super-conqueror*.[12] And we are—but not in our own strength. The love of Jesus—His love for us, not our love for Him—holds us, strengthens us, and makes us overcomers, unconquerable until the end.

> Who or what do you feel is against you? What do you fear might separate you from the love of God in Jesus? How do these verses comfort you? Be specific.

The Runaway Bunny is a children's book about a little bunny who wants to run away from his mother. But no matter where he thinks he might run, his mother finds a way to be with him and bring him home. Nothing could separate him from her love.

Romans 8 tells us the same thing. Nothing will separate us from our Father's love. God will pursue, find, hold, love, and bring us home.

Paul began chapter 8 with the assurance that there is no condemnation for those who are in Christ. He ended this glorious chapter with the fact that there is no separation, either. If you have been united to Christ, God loves you and will not let you fall. Suffering is real, but His love is stronger, and His glory is greater.

> Name three to five mercies you have seen in our passage this session.

> Work on your memory verses, praise God for His mercy, and glory in His promises.

DIGGING DEEPER
Check out these verses to help you better understand today's passage:
Isaiah 50:7-9 • John 16:33 • Hebrews 7:25

Session Six: THE SON AND THE SPIRIT INTERCEDE

WATCH Session Six video teaching.

1. The Spirit prays for us.

_____

_____

_____

_____

_____

_____

_____

_____

2. The Son prays for us.

_____

_____

_____

_____

_____

_____

_____

_____

DISCUSSION QUESTIONS

1   What day of personal study had the most impact on you? Why?

2   How did what you heard on the video teaching clarify, reinforce, or give new insight to what you studied this session?

3   What do you think it means to set your mind on the flesh and to set your mind on the Spirit? Which occupies the majority of your thoughts?

4   In what ways has the Spirit of God testified, or born witness, to your spirit that you are a child of God?

5   Describe how knowing that both the Spirit and the Son are interceding for you strengthens you.

6   What new mercies did you see in the passage this session?

7   What is the most significant thing you learned about God, the gospel, or yourself this session?

To access the video teaching sessions, use the instructions in the back of your Bible study book.

SESSION SEVEN

Mercy Humbles Us

ROMANS 9–11

Introduction

I've been to the Grand Canyon twice—once when I was thirteen and again two years ago. The first time I went, we stayed for three days and were able to ride mules partway down the canyon. The more recent visit was a mere twenty-four-hour stay, and we only had time to walk along the rim. I would love to go again and take the time to hike to the bottom of the canyon and then camp there a night or two before heading back to the top.

There are different ways to view the same thing. Some visits are long and allow you to linger, looking at all the details. Think of a slow hike, where you take the time to pick up individual rocks and smell flowers along the way. Other visits are relatively short, and the view is more like the one you get from an airplane—you can see the big picture, but not the details. Both views can be beautiful and beneficial.

If last session was like sitting on the summit of a great mountain, taking deep breaths of crisp air and viewing the vista of God's magnificent love, this session will be more like staying on the rim of the Grand Canyon, peering over the edge toward the depth below.

Romans 9–11 is a deep canyon and there is much to see. I hope you will stay for a longer visit in the future, taking time to turn over every rock. But this session we're only going to observe from the rim, focusing on the big picture of what we see.

MEMORY VERSES

> How then will they call on him in whom they have not believed? And how are they to believe in him of whom they have never heard? And how are they to hear without someone preaching? And how are they to preach unless they are sent? As it is written, "How beautiful are the feet of those who preach the good news!"

ROMANS 10:14-15

Prayer for the Week

Father, I bow before You as I open Your holy

Word. Please grant me greater understanding

and more humility to believe. Almighty God, You

are good; Your ways are good, and Your Word

is good. May my study this week make me more

grateful for my salvation and more eager to share

it with others. I ask this in Jesus' name, **Amen.**

SOVEREIGN MERCY

READ ROMANS 9:1-29.

For a Christian, few things in life cause more grief than loving someone who isn't yet saved. Whether it's a parent, spouse, child, sibling, or close friend, we long for those we love to know Jesus as Lord and Savior. And, if we're honest, we wonder when and if God will save them—and why He hasn't already.

Paul was wrestling with these same questions. As a Jewish man, he loved his people and longed for them to know Christ. His struggle with grief and wrestling to understand shows us what to do with our questions.

Today we're not going to move through our usual three questions—*What does it say? What does it mean?* and *What do I do?*—but, instead, simply ask questions as we progress through Paul's argument.

> **How did Paul express his grief in verses 2-3? Do you feel the same way about anybody? Explain.**

> **How would you summarize verses 1-5?**

Israel had been given everything. The Israelites were God's people. God had entered into a special relationship with them through the covenants. The Law and the prophets were theirs. They were physical descendants of Abraham. The Son of God took on flesh as a Jewish man and dwelt among Jewish people. If God was going to save anyone, shouldn't it be them?

Paul was going to remind himself and his readers that nobody is automatically saved because of family ties or because of a family heritage of faith. People are saved only because God, through Jesus, saves them.

A CLOSER LOOK

*"As it is written,
'Jacob, I loved, but
Esau I hated'" (Rom.
9:13).* It's startling to
read that God hated
Esau. But, rather
than "hate" meaning
God had an
intensely negative
feeling for Esau, it
simply means God
did not favor or set
His love on Esau like
He did on Jacob.

List the two Old Testament families Paul used as examples in verses 6–13. Write one thing Paul wanted us to know next to each example.

Isaac, not Ishmael, was the child of promise. Jacob, not Esau, was chosen by God. Neither Isaac nor Jacob was selected because of anything they had done but chosen before they were even born! This is hard to read and even harder to understand. We want to cry out, *But, God, that can't be right and doesn't seem fair!* Which is exactly what Paul predicted we'd say.

What question did Paul pose in verse 14? What was his immediate answer?

What objection did Paul predict in verse 19? What was his answer in verses 20–21?

Paul seemed to be reading our minds. As we read these hard verses, most of us wonder if God is being unjust or unfair. But Paul was quick to remind us of two fundamental truths: God is God, and we are not.

God is sovereign and has the right to run the world any way He pleases. He has the right to save whomever He wills. He is the Creator; we are the created. Or, as Paul said, God is the potter; we are simply the clay. (See vv. 19–24.)

When we are confronted with truths like these in Scripture, we have a choice in how we respond. We can shake our fists at God and demand He explain Himself. We can shrug our shoulders and walk away shaking our heads. Or we can bend our knees and bow our hearts before His sovereign wisdom.

Here's the reality of our situation. God has given each of us a brain that weighs approximately three pounds. Our brain is finite, fragile, and slowly failing. To be fair, He's given that three-pound, finite brain the ability to comprehend amazing things—and He calls us to use that little organ to know Him and love Him. But He has never promised us that we will be able to comprehend the totality of who He is or completely understand His ways. Because God is God and we are not, there will always be a point when our understanding reaches the limit, and we should simply bow before the mystery that remains.

What is your response to the previous paragraph? Do you agree or disagree? Explain.

According to these verses, circle the reasons listed that accurately answer the question, *Why did God save me?*

- because He loved me

- because I am a good person

- because of His purposes of election

- because of His mercy

- because of His compassion

- to display His power

- because I was baptized

- that His name might be proclaimed

- in order to make known the riches of His glory

If you are in Christ, you are a recipient of God's unfathomable mercy. Mercy is a free gift, bestowed on those to whom God freely chooses to show mercy. The question is not why doesn't God save everyone. The question is why does God save anyone—especially me? And the answer is His great mercy.

Write out any questions or thoughts you have about these verses. As you do, don't shake your fists or shrug your shoulders, but bow your knees and turn your thoughts into a prayer thanking God for saving you.

Our job is not to resolve all the tension we feel or answer all of the questions we have. Remember, we're just peering into this great canyon of mystery. But, ultimately, let us simply bow before our merciful God in humility, gratitude, and wonder.

DIGGING DEEPER
Check out these verses to help you better understand today's passage:
Deuteronomy 7:6-8 • Isaiah 55:8-9 • Ephesians 1:3-6

STRAIGHTFORWARD FAITH

READ ROMANS 9:30–10:13.

I have a friend who was raised as a Hindu. In college, while meeting with a campus minister, she told him that she thought of God as someone who was sitting on the top of a high mountain. All the different religions in the world were just diverse paths for people to climb up to him. The campus minister wisely agreed with her that it is as if God is on a high mountain. But he told her that, instead of us trying to make our way up to God, God actually came down to us.

In a nutshell, that's the difference between other world religions and Christianity. Either we have to climb our way up to God or God has to come to us. Either we earn and deserve salvation, or we receive it.

Which is it for you? Are you striving, working, climbing, trying to get to God? Oh, friend, rejoice in the truths of our passage today—salvation has come down.

What Does It Say?

We've seen over and over the centrality of righteousness, not just in Romans, but in our salvation. Paul described two paths toward righteousness in Romans 9:30-32. He used the Israelites to show one path and the Gentiles to show the other.

According to verses 30-32:

Who "pursued" righteousness?

What was the result?

Why?

The two ways to gain righteousness—striving or simply believing—are polar opposites in every way. We can make understanding this so hard when it's actually so simple.

> **According to Romans 10:9-10, answer the following questions:**
>
> **What does someone need to confess with her mouth?**
>
> **What does someone need to believe in her heart?**
>
> **What is the result of these combined actions?**
>
> **List all the words and phrases from verses 11-13 that show salvation is for all people.**

Now you might be wondering, *How is what we just learned today about our responsibility compatible with God's purposes and sovereignty over salvation that we studied yesterday?* Good question! Yesterday's passage looked at salvation from God's perspective; today's passage looks at it from ours.

There are many mysteries about God—the Trinity and the simultaneous full humanity and full deity of Jesus, to name just two. Another of the big mysteries is that God is completely sovereign, and humans have full responsibility. We're not puppets. We have agency that God respects. How are we to hold those two truths in tension?

Now would be a good time for me to remind us about our brains. How much do they weigh? How long do they last? There are just some things we are not going to fully comprehend this side of glory. We are limited creatures, and God is an infinite being. Thank goodness we're not saved because we understand; we're saved because we believe.

At the same time, we are called to know what we are capable of knowing. We're called to love God with all our minds (Matt. 22:37), be transformed by the renewing of our minds (Rom. 12:2), and set our minds on the things of God (Col. 3:2). The Israelites are condemned in this passage for having a zeal without knowledge and an ignorance of the righteousness of God (Rom. 10:2-3). So, while we can't understand everything about God, let's heartily apply our minds to what we can know.

What Does It Mean?

Zeal is often prioritized over knowledge. We hear (and say) things like, "As long as I am sincere, I'll be OK with God." Or, "My heart is in the right place." But it's not just how we feel, it's also what we know. God desires that we grow in our knowledge of Him. In the same way that I want to grow in knowledge of my husband—knowing what blesses him, what he thinks, who he is—I want to grow in my knowledge of the Lord. And I want my zeal for the Lord to be based on that knowledge.

From what Paul said about the Israelites in this passage, why is it dangerous to have zeal without knowledge?

How do you see this playing out in our world/culture today?

List some things you have learned about the Lord that have produced zeal in you.

Considering all you have learned about righteousness in Romans so far, how would you explain the three phrases used to describe the Israelites' relationship with righteousness in verse 3?

"Being ignorant of the righteousness of God"

"Seeking to establish their own [righteousness]"

"Did not submit to God's righteousness"

What Do I Do?

The first thing we need to do is ask ourselves if we have confessed with our mouths that Jesus is Lord and believed in our hearts that God raised Him from the dead! Have you? If you have or if you do, the result is clear and sure—you will be saved.

How could you use verse 3 to explain the gospel to someone of another faith?

How could you use verses 9-13 to share the gospel with someone?

Jesus, and the simplicity of the salvation He offers, was a stumbling stone to the Jews. But for those of us who cast ourselves on Jesus, He is the Rock of our salvation. We don't have to climb up because Jesus came down. He has done it all. Salvation is a beautiful gift we receive, not a reward we earn.

DIGGING DEEPER
Check out these verses to help you better understand today's passage:
Deuteronomy 30:11-14 • Isaiah 28:16 • 2 Corinthians 1:20

JOYFUL PROCLAMATION

READ ROMANS 10:14-21.

I remember the first time I really heard the message of the gospel. I was in middle school at my church's weeklong summer camp. Around a campfire one night, the visiting youth pastor explained the gospel and how salvation is found only in Christ. God gave me ears to hear; I believed, called on the name of the Lord, and was saved.

We all have to first hear the message of the gospel before we can respond to the message of the gospel. Paul ended yesterday's passage with the great words, "For 'everyone who calls on the name of the Lord will be saved'" (v. 13). And to that we say, "Hallelujah and amen!" It's good to be reminded that salvation is for all people.

But Paul's statement should lead the attentive reader to ask a follow-up question: *How will people know to call on the name of the Lord?* Which, in typical Paul fashion, is exactly what he anticipated his readers would ask.

What Does It Say?

In verses 13-15, Paul laid out a series of events, starting with the last and most important one—calling on the Lord.

> Write the chain of events found in verses 13-15 chronologically (in the order of how they would actually happen). Underline the actions that only God can do. Circle the ones that you and I can do.

We mentioned back in Session Two that Paul hoped the church in Rome would join him in taking the gospel to the far-reaches of Spain (Rom. 15:24). The worldwide proclamation of the gospel then, just as now, required individuals ready and willing to proclaim the gospel as well as churches ready and willing to send. There are always people who need to hear the good news of Jesus Christ!

One thing we see in this passage is Paul's passion for going and preaching. But he knew that not everyone who heard his message would call on the name of the Lord.

What different responses to the gospel do you see in today's passage?

It's important to remember that we, as believers, are responsible for sharing the gospel. We're not responsible for how people respond to the gospel. Some will reject God. Some will joyfully receive Him. Then there will be others who we think will never come to Christ, but they surprise us and call on Him. So we pray and ask God to give open ears and soft hearts to those we are sharing the good news with.

What Does It Mean?

Why would the feet of those who preach the good news be considered beautiful? By whom?

What do we learn about God in Romans 10:21? Use all the words you can think of to describe God's posture toward those who don't know Him pictured in this verse.

God holds out His hands to people who reject Him. This is amazingly great news for those of us who love someone who appears to be rejecting God! He is patient, merciful, kind, compassionate, and willing to reach out to those who are running from Him.

We also see that this time of God holding out His "hands to a disobedient and contrary people" with His offer of salvation will come to an end (v. 21). Today is the day to go, proclaim, and pray that those hearing will believe and call to the One holding His hands out to them. Today is the day to believe.

What Do I Do?

How can your answer to the first question of the day shape the way you:

Pray for yourself about sharing the gospel?

Pray for others who also need to be sharing the gospel?

Pray for those hearing the gospel?

How has verse 20 been true of God in your life?

Who shared the gospel with you? If that person is still living, consider making a call or sending a note, text, or email to express your gratefulness for his or her faithfulness.

Is there someone in your life who has not called on the Lord Jesus Christ? If so, has he or she heard of Him? Could it be that you are being sent to that person? Ask the Lord to give you feet willing to go, a mouth willing to speak, and words that clearly tell the good news of Jesus Christ. Ask the Lord to give that person ears to hear and a heart to believe so that his or her mouth will confess that Jesus is Lord. Ask the Lord to give saving faith as he or she hears the word of Christ from you.

DIGGING DEEPER
Check out these verses to help you better understand today's passage:
Matthew 9:37-38 • Matthew 13:4-8 • Matthew 28:18-20

FAITHFUL REMNANT

READ ROMANS 11:1-10.

Paul Harvey, a radio broadcaster during the second half of the twentieth century, is perhaps best known for his series, *The Rest of the Story*. During those broadcasts, Harvey would tell a story but withhold a key piece of information. When the missing piece of information was given, his listeners would be astounded and the whole story would immediately make sense. At the end of the tale, he would announce, "And now you know the rest of the story."[1]

In so many ways, we are like Harvey's listeners. We live our lives not knowing the rest of the story—or at least not knowing the whole story. We don't see the all-encompassing, eternal scope of God's plans and purposes. We live in just a brief slice of the story.

Because we don't see it all, we can be prone to doubt. And, if this slice that we see isn't playing out exactly as we think it should, we might be tempted to question whether or not God is faithful, trustworthy, and a keeper of His word. Paul—the apostle, not Harvey—figured we'd ask as much.

What Does It Say?

The church in Rome, composed of Jewish and Gentile believers, realized many, many Jewish people had not believed Jesus was the Messiah. The realization was unsettling because if God had rejected Israel, His chosen people, would He reject them, the newly constituted people of God, as well? The big questions were: *Will God be faithful to His people, and will He fulfill His promises?* And the beautiful answer is: *Absolutely!*

What question did Paul ask in verse 1? How did he answer it in verses 1-2?

Paul used two examples to prove his point. First, he used himself. Then, he appealed to Elijah.

> Recalling what you know about Paul (see pp. 13–17), why was he such a great example of the fact that God had not rejected His people and the truth of verses 5-6?

> Elijah thought he was the only faithful follower left. But how many were there?

> On what basis was God faithful (vv. 5-6)?

In so many ways Paul was restating what he already said in Romans 9—God does not save people based on family ties or a family heritage of faith. People are saved because God is full of grace, and because of that grace, He saves a people for Himself.

What Does It Mean?

By using himself as an example in verse 1, Paul wanted his readers to see that anyone, even those with the hardest of hearts toward God, can be saved. And as God reminded Elijah, God might be saving more people than we think He is. So, if you are praying for someone with a hard heart or you don't see many new people coming to faith, don't give up hope. God is at work!

> Romans 11:7 categorizes two types of Israelites. What are the categories, and into which group does the remnant, described in verses 4-5, fit?

We're back to that word we discussed in Session Six, Day Four—*elect*. Before you answer the next question, turn back to page 129 and refresh your understanding of the two major schools of thought on foreknowledge, predestination, and election. And remind yourself that there are some tensions in God's Word that will not be fully resolved in our minds this side of glory.

> What further insight do verses 5-7 shed on the concept of election? Where in verses 7-10 do you see the tension between God's sovereignty and man's responsibility?

When Paul wrote that "the rest were hardened" (v. 7), he meant by God. And the hardening was both because they had tried to "establish their own [righteousness]" (10:3), not pursuing it by faith, but rather by works (9:32), and also because God "will have mercy on whom [He will] have mercy" (9:15). God did not open their eyes and ears, and, at the same time, they refused to see or hear. It was their fault, and it was the work of God. Confusing? Yes! But, as one commentator wrote, "The Bible is not very interested in resolving our philosophical puzzle as to how these can be true at one and the same time."[2]

> What do you think it means to "have eyes that would not see" and "ears that would not hear" (11:8)? In what ways do these verses remind you of Romans 2?

As we've seen throughout Romans, Paul continued to show that, of all the peoples of the earth, the Israelites should have been the first ones to run to Jesus. They had the covenants, the promises, the patriarchs, the Law, and the prophets. But, for the most part, they rejected Jesus, the One to whom all of these things pointed. In the same way, there will be people who are exposed to church, God's Word, and the gospel message who will not be saved.

What Do I Do?

The story about Elijah that Paul referenced is found in 1 Kings 18–19. In a spectacular showdown at Mount Carmel, Elijah called upon the Lord to show His power over the prophets of Baal. The confrontation was a dramatic and decisive victory for God through Elijah. (Go read it if you haven't!) However, immediately after this great triumph, Elijah ran away and despaired of his own life. In spite of how miraculously God had just shown up, Elijah thought he was alone and the only remaining person in all of Israel who was faithful to the Lord.

Elijah was far from alone. God quickly told him that He had kept for Himself seven thousand men! I don't know if Elijah was indulging self-pity (i.e. "poor me") or if he was experiencing spiritual pride (i.e. "I'm the only faithful follower of Yahweh"), but God wanted Elijah, who couldn't see the whole story, to know that He, God, was at work in both big, dramatic ways as well as in small, unseen ways. The same is true today.

Like Elijah, you might feel as if you're the only person in your family or circle of friends whom God has saved. Or maybe you think you are one of the only people you know who faithfully keeps the Word of God. What we need to see from these verses is those thoughts are not true. Why? Because God is at work all around us, in big, dramatic ways as well as in small, unseen ways. Remember, we don't see the whole story.

Do you ever feel alone in your faith, in your ministry, or in your desire to follow God? How do these verses both correct and encourage you?

Is there a person you think is too hard-hearted to be saved? Or someone who seems blind and deaf to the gospel message? Write a prayer for that person, asking God to, by His grace and because of His mercy, give that person eyes to see and ears to hear. Commit to praying this prayer for this person for a specific period of time.

DIGGING DEEPER
Check out these verses to help you better understand today's passage:
1 Samuel 12:22 • Ephesians 2:8-10 • 2 Timothy 2:13

GLORY FOREVER

READ ROMANS 11:11-36.

Before we dive into today's passage, let me remind us of where we are. We're leaning over the edge of a huge canyon, staring into its marvelous depths. And, because we're not hiking to the bottom, our observations will be limited. But that's OK; we will still see beauty and wonders galore!

The verses we will study today are some of the hardest to understand in all of Romans. But that doesn't mean we need to shy away from them. Every verse in the Bible has been given to us so that we can know God. What it does mean is that we need to approach these verses with humility and a desire to learn what God wants us to know. Like we did in Day One, we're going to set our usual three questions—*What does it say? What does it mean?* and *What do I do?*—aside and just progress through the verses.

Paul's main point in these verses was to remind his readers that our current reality is not the end of the story and that all believers, especially Gentile believers, should be full of gratitude and humility that God's grace has come to us.

The situation the believers in Rome were currently experiencing—that more Gentiles than Jews were following Christ—was not the end of the story. God had made promises to Israel and had not forgotten them. He was still at work.

Within the nation of Israel, there had always been those who followed God and those who didn't. There were faithful Jews and unfaithful Jews in both the Old Testament and the New. In the same way, as we've mentioned before, there are those who go to church (are visibly seen as part of God's people) who are not saved. We should be encouraged that God is not finished with them yet, either.

Read verses 16-24.

What is the main metaphor used in verses 17-24?

Who do you think each of the following represent?

The root:

The natural branches:

The wild branches:

What should the response of the Gentile believers be? What are the two ways Paul phrased that response (vv. 18,20)?

What connects the wild branch to the root (v. 20)?

Whether we're a natural branch (Jewish) or one that has been grafted in (Gentile), the only way to have eternal life is by being vitally connected to the root (Jesus). The root is what nourishes, strengthens, and sustains a branch, no matter what kind of branch it is.

In verse 22, Paul asked his readers to consider two aspects of God's character: His kindness and His severity. Where in verses 16-24 do you see evidence of both?

Do you tend to think about or prioritize one of these characteristics over the other? Explain.

Where have you seen both God's kindness and His severity in your life?

It's normal to focus more on God's kindness than on His severity. But the severity of God is similar to His judgment—a good thing that our hearts actually yearn for. If God is only kind, then the evil, sin, and wickedness in our world would go unpunished. But if God were only severe, we would all perish. I am eternally grateful that God will both destroy the wickedness in me and around me and, at the same time, that our Almighty God is so abundantly kind.

Paul used the word *continue* (some translations say *remain*) twice in two verses (22,23). What happens to each group if it doesn't "continue"?

Paul was not saying a true believer can be cut off. That would mean the gospel message is: receive salvation by grace alone, through faith alone, in Christ alone—but remain in your salvation by your own good efforts. No! It's not that we are strong enough to hold on. God is the strong One who holds on to us. So, those who don't "continue" in the faith were never really saved to begin with.

Our continuance, or perseverance to the end, is proof that God has really saved us and is the One who has been holding us fast every single day. And the grace that holds us fast is the same grace that can take those who no longer "continue in their unbelief" and truly graft them into the folds of faith (v. 23).

The next section contains a verse that has caused much debate—verse 26, "And in this way all Israel will be saved." I think it's helpful to make a few comments about the following three words:

- *All*: as in many other places in Scripture, the word *all* can mean "a great many" rather than "every single one." (See Luke 8:37; Luke 15:1; John 8:2; John 13:35.)

- *Israel*: because Paul had been talking about ethnic Israel, there's no reason to think he has now switched to any other meaning.

- *Saved*: salvation is always and only through faith in Jesus Christ. Nobody, including the Jewish people, can or will be saved any other way.

   What two words appear four times each in Romans 11:30-32? Describe the relationship between the two.

What can we take away from our passages this session?

- Our God is kind and shows mercy to disobedient people (like you and me).

- God is at work in every age of history. He is at work now redeeming and saving a people for Himself—even hard-hearted and rebellious people.

- We should all be humble—Gentile Christians most of all. Salvation is a gift of God and should not make us proud, but grateful.

- God is faithful to His Word and His people. We should pray for the salvation of our Jewish friends and neighbors.

These truths—hard to understand, yet gloriously true—didn't cause Paul to shake his fists or shrug his shoulders. They caused him to worship.

Read Romans 11:33-36 again. Paul praised God for being so much wiser than we are.

Choose two to three words or phrases that stand out to you in this beautiful hymn of praise. List them below, along with the reason you chose them. Then spend some time in prayer praising God using those words.

Name three to five mercies you have seen in our passage this session.

I hope you have been encouraged by God's Word this week as we have peered over the rim into the unsearchable and inscrutable depths of His wisdom and mercy. To Him, truly, be glory forever.

DIGGING DEEPER
Check out these verses to help you better understand today's passage:
Exodus 34:5-8 • Ezekiel 37:1-14 • John 15:1-11

Session Seven: BURSTING FORTH WITH PRAISE

WATCH Session Seven video teaching.

1. The riches of God

2. The wisdom and knowledge of God

3. Unsearchable and inscrutable

DISCUSSION QUESTIONS

1 What day of personal study had the most impact on you? Why?

2 How did what you heard on the video teaching clarify, reinforce, or give new insight to what you studied this session?

3 In Romans 10:9, why do you think Paul used each of the following phrases to describe how someone is saved? What is the significance of each?

   • "Confess with your mouth that Jesus is Lord"

   • "Believe in your heart that God raised him from the dead"

4 Do you ever feel alone in your faith, in your ministry, or in your desire to follow God? In what ways did your study this session both correct and encourage you?

5 In what ways have you experienced both God's kindness and severity in your life?

6 What new mercies did you see in the passage this session?

7 What is the most significant thing you learned about God, the gospel, or yourself this session?

To access the video teaching sessions, use the instructions in the back of your Bible study book.

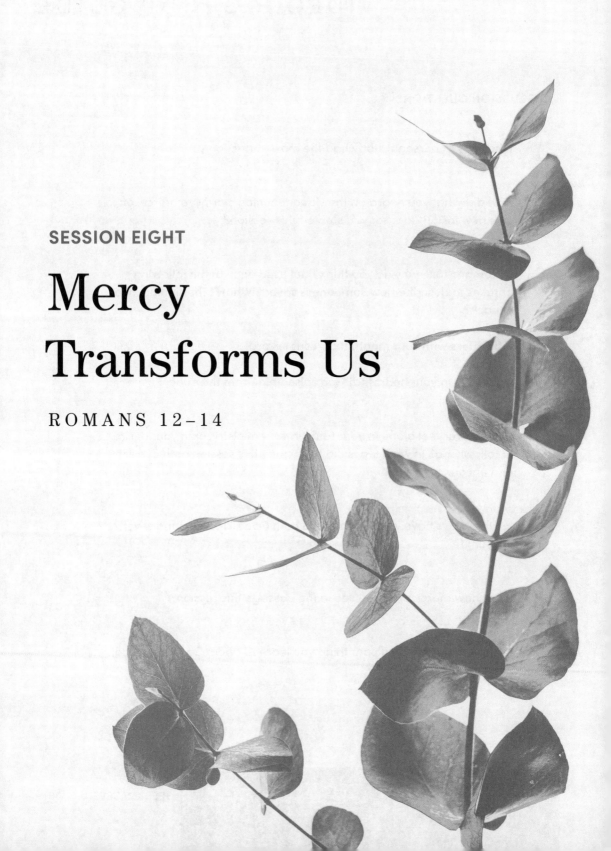

Mercy Transforms Us

ROMANS 12–14

Introduction

Growing up, if my brother and I were unkind to each other, we knew that not only would we receive a consequence, but also a lengthy lecture reminding us of all the reasons why we should be kind. The reasons were given to help us not only change our behavior, but also, hopefully, lead us to change our hearts. My parents wanted us to know why kindness was important and, as a result, hoped we would have a greater desire for kindness that would lead to us actually being kind. Because knowledge—what we know—is meant to inform behavior—how we live.

In Romans 1–11, Paul focused on what we are to know. He carefully laid out the beautiful truths of how the gospel is the power of God for salvation. We've spent the last seven sessions looking at this glorious gospel in great detail. We've learned about the pervasive nature of sin and the depths of unrighteousness. We've also seen the multiple, magnificent mercies of God extended to us through faith in Jesus. As a result, we have peace, hope, joy, victory over sin, comfort, surety, eternal security, and everlasting love. We noted God's sovereignty over salvation and the depth of the mystery of His wisdom. After laying out glorious truth after glorious truth, Paul bowed in wonder and worship at the end of Romans 11.

Now, as we turn the page to Romans 12, the focus shifts from the truths we are to know to the way we are to live. I say this all the time: the Bible is meant not only to inform us, but also to transform us. The gospel message isn't just meant to ensure our eternal future; it's meant to change our present reality.

Oh, the glorious truths matter! God wants us to know these truths, believe them, share them with others, speak them back to our own souls, and rest deeply in them—and live differently as a result. God doesn't just want your Sunday mornings or your half-hearted worship. He wants all of you—mind, body, and soul. He wants your heads (what you know), your hearts (what you love), and your hands (what you do).

Paul will spend the rest of Romans showing us what a life and a church transformed by the gospel of grace look like. He's going to show us how to live the moments of our days in light of the magnificent mercies of God. Because of this change in focus, we're going to stop asking our standard three questions each day and simply ask the last one: *What do I do?*

MEMORY VERSES

> Therefore, brothers and sisters, in view of the mercies of God, I urge you to present your bodies as a living sacrifice, holy and pleasing to God; this is your true worship. Do not be conformed to this age, but be transformed by the renewing of your mind, so that you may discern what is the good, pleasing, and perfect will of God.

ROMANS 12:1-2 (CSB)

Prayer for the Week

Almighty God, You are the King of glory! You are the only wise God, merciful, gracious, slow to anger, and abounding in steadfast love and faithfulness. You have showered Your love and mercy on me. Please show me how to respond to Your love, how to live in light of Your mercy, and how to display Your glory to a world that desperately needs to see You. Please meet me in the study of Your Word this week. Transform every part of me in such a profound way that I live the moments of my days in proper response to Your amazing grace. In Jesus' name, **Amen.**

DAY 1

SERVE ONE ANOTHER

READ ROMANS 12:1-8.

The first two verses of today's passage are not only your memory verses, but also the summary of all that is to come. And they contain the title words of this study—*in view of God's mercies*. They are important, rich verses worthy of lingering over. Though we'll just touch on them in today's work, they will be our focus in the video teaching for this session.

> In verse 1, what command did Paul give, and what was the reason or basis for it? What do you think both the command and the reason might mean?

Different Bible translations offer slightly different ways of wording the phrase in verse 1, "by the mercies of God' (ESV, NKJV, RSV). The NIV says, 'in view of God's mercy" and the CSB says, "in view of the mercies of God." The title of this study stuck more closely with the CSB for two important reasons. First, the Greek word for *mercy* is plural—Paul wanted us to think of the many, multiple mercies of God that Paul expounded.[1] Second, we don't present our bodies just by God's mercies, but because of them. His mercies shown to us in His gospel of grace are the reason we offer ourselves as living sacrifices. This is the right response to all He has done for us. So everything Paul is about to tell us regarding how to live as followers of Christ is done in view of, or because of, God's great mercies.

> On the last days of the previous sessions, you were asked to name three to five mercies you had seen in our passages those sessions. To note the vast mercies of God, go back through your study and capture your answers here.

What do you think it looks like to "not be conformed to this world" (v. 2)? What are we to be instead, and what are some specific ways we can do that?

Are you familiar with the phrase, "when the rubber meets the road"? We use it to refer to the time when action begins, when ideas start to take effect in daily life. Well, in these verses, Paul showed us how the rubber meets the road—how all of the glorious truths he'd written should be pressed into the moments of our days.

In verse 3, Paul used a double exhortation about how we are and are not to think about ourselves. List each exhortation and write what you think each means. What are some practical ways you can do both of these?

A CLOSER LOOK
The gift of prophecy:
The prophets in the Old Testament (and the apostles in the New Testament) spoke for God and their words carried His authority. Often, they revealed a future event. But since we are neither Old Testament prophets nor New Testament apostles, prophecy here most likely means some type of instructing, explaining, and encouraging others publicly with the truth of Scripture. This type of prophecy explains the truths of Scripture and is under the authority of the Word and the leadership of the local church. It is "forth-telling" rather than foretelling.

In verses 4-5, Paul compared the church to a body, an analogy he also used in other letters. Why is this such a great illustration? How integral do you view your part in the body of your local church?

Humility and interdependence are essential for our Christian life and growth. Commitment to our local church is a vital part of following Jesus. He established His church. He loves His church. And He's coming back for His church. We are meant to live our faith out in the context of Christian community—like members of a body, intricately joined together, many but one, different functions but the same overall purpose.

Make a list of the seven gifts Paul mentioned in verses 6-8 and describe how each gift can be used to serve others.

This list of gifts is not exhaustive. The Bible mentions numerous other spiritual gifts (see today's "Digging Deeper"), but all are given and empowered by the Spirit, meant to be used heartily and in service to others.

Is your spiritual gift in this list? If so, how are you using it to help your church carry out its purpose?

If your gift is not listed here, what do you think your spiritual gift is/might be?

What are some things that can keep you from using your spiritual gifts?

As you work on your memory verse today, think about each phrase and consider why it is important as we step into this new part of Romans. Ask God to help you recount and recall His mercies as He shows you how to live in light of them.

DIGGING DEEPER
Check out these verses to help you better understand today's passage:
1 Corinthians 12:7-10 • Ephesians 4:11-17 • Hebrews 13:15-17

LOVE ONE ANOTHER

READ ROMANS 12:9-21.

If you were to have a conversation with someone who had never met a Christian and that person asked you, "What does a Christian look like? How would I know one if I saw one?" how would you answer? Or if the question was, "What is the difference between your church and my book club?" what would you say?

Paul gave us our answer. It's love. Love—genuine, affectionate, patient, humble, and fervent love for each other—should be the defining mark of a Christian and the church. But true love is not just kindness or warm feelings. True love is hard and involves concrete action.

Paul revealed the character of love by describing what love does and does not do. Using the following chart, list four to five of the positive commands (what love is or does) on the left side and four to five of the negative ones (what love is not or does not do) on the right. Choose one command from the left column and one from the right column and write down ways you can grow in this particular way of showing love.

Love Is/Does	Love Is Not/Does Not
Example: Love is genuine.	Example: Love is not slothful.
Ways I can grow:	Ways I can grow:

Which of these characteristics of love best describes your church? How can you help create or nurture this culture of love in your church?

Depending on your age, you might have heard the song "They'll Know We Are Christians." (If not, Google it and listen.) It makes some bold claims about the genuineness of our love for each other and the witness that love provides. But can we sing it and truly mean it? Will others really know we are Christians by our love?

Social media allows others to literally listen in on the conversations between Christians. Sadly, in far too many cases, I'm not sure those conversations would convince anyone that love is meant to be our defining mark.

If you spend time on social media, how do the following phrases from Romans 12 challenge you and why? (If you're not on social media, you can answer the question based on the letters you write, texts you send, or conversations you have.)

"Outdo one another in showing honor"

"Bless those who persecute you"

"Rejoice with those who rejoice"

"Weep with those who weep"

"Live in harmony with one another"

"Never be wise in your own sight"

Because we live in a broken world full of broken people (ourselves included), broken relationships plague us all. But not only do they grieve us, they grieve God. Verse 18 gives us both an exhortation and comfort as we navigate broken relationships.

What was Paul's instruction in verse 18?

What were the caveats to this instruction?

Is there someone you're struggling to live at peace with? Explain.

Paul called us to live at peace with everyone—however he recognized that, this side of glory, peace may not be attainable. But let's not move too quickly to the "if possible," and "so far as it depends on you" phrases and breathe a sigh of relief thinking, *Well, I've done everything I can. The ball is in her court now.* Instead, let's stop and reassess.

Have you really done everything you can to live at peace with that certain person? Do these verses offer any ways to move toward that person in love?

Spend some time in prayer for that certain person (or people). Ask God to show you if there are ways you can move in peace toward that person again. If peace is not possible at this time, ask God to comfort your soul and leave the door of your heart open for reconciliation. Journal your prayer and any action steps you can take.

For most of us, it's probably easier to weep with those who weep than it is to rejoice with those who rejoice. Envy, comparison, and coveting can prevent us from feeling true joy in the successes, gifts, and blessings others receive.

How does today's passage either convict or encourage you to love others by rejoicing with them?

A CLOSER LOOK
"Heap burning coals on his head" (Rom. 12:20).
There are two main ways to interpret this hard-to-understand phrase. In the first, the coals represent shame on the part of the one carrying them. In other words, when a Christian shows kindness to an enemy, the enemy may end up feeling ashamed for his or her evil actions and repent. In the second interpretation, the coals represent God's judgment, and the point is that when we show kindness to our enemies, we do so because we know that God will eventually judge all evil deeds. Ultimately though, we hope our kindness will lead our enemies to repentance, but if it doesn't, we know that God will one day make all wrongs right.

In this passage, Paul talked about the importance of love as a personal character virtue in every believer. He showed how that virtue is to be displayed with other believers. But he also instructed us on how to love anyone, whether inside the church or not, who might hate or malign you.

These commands in verses 19-21—to do good to our enemies—are the most radical, counter-cultural, counter-intuitive commands we could imagine. When we are wronged, payback, revenge, and cancel culture are our natural responses. We cannot do what God is asking of us in our own strength, our own wisdom, or our own initiative. This response has to be a work of the Spirit. But that's the beautiful thing. When the Spirit enables you to love like God loves, it's a powerful witness to the watching world.

In what ways do these verses describe how God has loved us?

Is there someone who has wronged you? In what ways do you desire to seek revenge? Do you replay the hurt over and over in your mind? Do you envision what "sweet revenge" would look like? Using the commands in these verses, make a list of four to five ways you could practically, radically, only-by-the-Spirit love that person. Ask God to give you the humility and grace to do it.

This kind of love is a far cry from the passive "kumbaya" that many think is the way Christians are to love. This kind of love is hard. But as Christians, this is the kind of love we have received! Jesus loves us with a brotherly affection. He has blessed us even though we have persecuted Him. Jesus loves us, His former enemies. And Jesus overcame all evil with good.

We don't love like this on our own. We can't. But because we have been united to Jesus and His perfect love, we are changed into people who can show supernatural, uncommon love to not only our brothers and sisters in Christ, but also to those who don't yet know Him. May they all know we are Christians by our love.

DIGGING DEEPER
Check out these verses to help you better understand today's passage:
Luke 6:27-31 • John 13:34-35 • 1 Corinthians 13:1-7

DAY 3

SUBMIT TO ONE ANOTHER

READ ROMANS 13:1-14.

I love dogs. When my children were growing up, we had a rotating pack of three dogs. The last pack of three was comprised of a German Shepherd, Fritz, who quietly ruled the roost; a Corgi mutt, Buddy, that was scrappy and kept the other dogs in line; and a docile Golden Retriever, Jeffery, whose main responsibility seemed to be to love everyone and everything. But Jeffery was an odd dog. His main oddity was what seemed to be an inordinate desire to submit to the other dogs. He would go out of his way to come before them and lie down. He would roll over when the other dogs walked by. It was borderline uncomfortable to watch. Why? Because willing submission feels like a foreign trait to most of us.

If you were raised in a western, North American culture (like me), you probably find even the topic of submission a bit uncomfortable. Most of us have been taught from an early age to cherish our rights, stand up for ourselves, and not let anyone walk all over us. Submission feels like the opposite of the rugged individualism, self-sufficiency, and complete independence many of us have been taught to hold as ideals.

But biblical submission isn't just rolling over and being a doormat. When God calls us to submit to one another and to those in authority over us, He always reminds us that it is ultimately Him we are submitting to. God calls us, not to rugged independence, but to total dependence on Him and beautiful interdependence on each other. And He calls us to submit to different types of authorities in our lives—willingly and cheerfully. Maybe we have something to learn from Jeffery after all.

> **Write down three to five words that describe what you think submission means.**

> **Paul gave multiple reasons for why we are to submit to governing authorities. Write down all you can find.**

We might read verses 1-7 and think Paul just couldn't foresee what it would be like to live in the twenty-first century under our current political culture. There is so much division, distrust, and disillusionment with most of the governments around the world. If Paul had understood our world, surely he wouldn't have written that the governing authorities have been instituted by God (v. 1), are God's servants (v. 4), and God's ministers (v. 6).

But guess who was emperor of the Roman empire during the time Paul wrote to the church in Rome? Nero—arguably one of the cruelest dictators the world has ever known. He murdered his own mother, beat his pregnant wife to death, and is allegedly responsible for starting the fire that burned Rome in AD 64—all for his own entertainment. Nero was particularly cruel to Christians. He sent many to their death, putting them on stakes and setting them on fire to use as "streetlights." Paul's political culture was definitely a bit more difficult than ours.

Yet, he called the church in Rome to submit. Was Paul advocating for submission in all things? No, and we know this by taking the whole counsel of God's Word into account. When the Sanhedrin told Peter and the other apostles to stop preaching Christ, they famously replied, "We must obey God rather than men" (Acts 5:29). If any authority requires you to disobey God, you are not to submit to that demand. If any authority asks you to do something against your Christian conscience, you do not have to submit to that request. Even though God has instituted all authorities, not all authorities use their power for good. Many use it for outright evil, and we are not called to fulfill evil demands. So our submission is limited.

But most of us aren't facing situations where submission to governing authorities would require us to disobey God's Word. Instead, most of us trivialize God's Word in order to disobey the governing authorities. Let's just take, for instance, laws around driving: don't speed, text, or drink and drive.

> According to these verses, what response should Christians have to the speed limit? To laws about texting while driving? To drinking and driving? In what ways do you struggle to submit? Why? Which verses are particularly convicting?

Remember, this passage is under the larger umbrella of how we are to love others.

In what ways is submission to authority in the driving laws mentioned in the previous question a way for Christians to love their neighbors? Be specific. What other areas can you think of?

Paul told us to pay what we owe others—taxes, revenue, respect, and honor—but then told us there is a debt we will never pay off—the debt of love. Meaning, we owe each other love. Every day. We never finish owing love to one another.

In verses 8 and 10, what reason did Paul give for paying off this ongoing debt of love? In verse 9, he used four of the ten commandments to illustrate his point. In what ways is keeping each of these ultimately keeping the commandment to love your neighbor as yourself?

Do not commit adultery:

Do not murder:

Do not steal:

Do not covet:

Love doesn't murder, steal, covet, or commit adultery (among many other things)—because true love sacrificially seeks the good of the other person. Adultery, regardless of any claims of love, is deeply harmful to the other person and motivated by selfish desire, not "true love." Murder and stealing obviously physically and materially harm the other person. Coveting robs us of the ability to seek the good of others because when we are jealous and want what they have, we want them to have less good things, not more.

Do you ever grow weary of loving others? Or tired of doing good? Weariness causes us to lose sight of the big picture and, when we do, living life in view of God's mercies can be hard. So Paul gave one of the most beautiful rally cries in all of Scripture: Wake up; the night is over; the dawn has broken, and salvation is at hand!

Make a list of both the positive commands (do this) and negative commands (don't do this) found in verses 11-14. If Paul gave a reason for the command, write it beside the instruction.

How does knowing salvation is nearer today than it was yesterday help you live faithfully and love deeply?

I love that Paul ended this passage with the command to put on Christ. Jesus covers us, clothes us in His righteousness, and arrays us with His beauty. We don't muster up good deeds and love for other people on our own. No, we put on Christ and walk in His love, remembering that we will see Him face-to-face very, very soon.

DIGGING DEEPER
Check out these verses to help you better understand today's passage:
Exodus 20:1-17 • 1 Peter 2:13-17 • 1 John 4:19

DAY 4

WELCOME ONE ANOTHER

READ ROMANS 14:1-12.

Oh, today's passage has a word for us! If we, in the body of Christ, would understand and obey what Paul told us here, I am convinced our churches, our witness, and our walks with the Lord would grow. Those are some mighty claims, I know, but the tribalism that haunts the modern church hinders our growth individually and corporately. In these verses, Paul commands unity in a type of diversity we rarely talk about—diversity of conviction.

Paul was addressing believers, those justified by faith. This is important because the divisions he addressed are not matters of salvation or orthodoxy; they're matters of Christian conscience. And there is freedom for diversity of conviction among true believers.

A CLOSER LOOK

Christian liberty means that if Scripture is silent in an area and does not expressly command, forbid, or instruct, we have the freedom, in Christ, to discern what to do. That discernment should be led by the Holy Spirit, informed by the whole counsel of God's Word, and seek to honor God. The passage we're studying is about what to do with our convictions, especially when we don't agree with others on the issue at hand.

List three to five words or phrases that let you know Paul is addressing believers.

To the best of your ability, describe the situation in the church at Rome. Who are the two groups, and what did they each believe?

Group One	Group Two

In these verses, we gain more insight into one of the issues that caused conflict and division between believers in the church in Rome. It appears there were differing opinions regarding what to eat and how to observe the religious calendar. The first group (Paul labeled them the "weak"), presumably composed of mostly Jewish Christians, felt uncomfortable eating certain food (most likely meat that was left over from a pagan sacrifice). Their Christian consciences led them to believe that eating certain foods would be dishonoring to the Lord. It wasn't that they believed their obedience made them right with God, they simply wanted to honor Him, to please Him, and believed that abstaining from certain foods would do so. They had the freedom to come to this conclusion.

The other group was composed primarily of Gentile Christians. They knew God had declared all food clean and were convinced of their freedom in matters of what to eat and how to observe the holidays. Technically, they were correct (Mark 7:19; Acts 10:15). But instead of loving their brothers and sisters, they were passing judgment on them because the "weak" didn't share their understanding of Christian liberty. They had the freedom to hold their conviction, but what they did with that conviction was wrong.

> How did Paul command each group to respond to the other (Rom. 14:1,3,10)? What reasons did he give for these actions?

> According to verse 6, what was motivating each group in their convictions?

Paul's argument can be confusing because of the words he used. He described those with a stronger, stricter, or more sensitive conscience as the weaker brother or sister. He called those with a more liberated conscience, those who felt more freedom in their convictions, strong. This feels counterintuitive to us because we value a strong conscience. And we should. But Paul wanted us to see that while there are numerous important issues in the church, not all are essential to the gospel. The weaker brother or sister is not the one with a strong conscience about essential things (which is good), but the one with an unnecessarily strong conscience about non-essential matters.

Paul was more concerned with how the Christians in Rome treated each other than he was with resolving their differences. Oh, sisters, we need to learn this lesson! Christians will always have a diversity of convictions around issues not essential to the gospel of grace. For instance, the church, in the not-so-distant past, experienced a diversity of convictions around dancing and whether or not women should wear pants or makeup—some thought dancing, pants, and makeup were not pleasing to God. Others felt their Christian freedom liberated them from these restrictions. These issues, while important to some, were not central to the gospel in any way. Instead of obeying the way of Romans 14, many churches and denominations split over these differences in non-essential matters. How much damage have we, as the church, caused over these types of quarrels?

> Identify two to four non-essential issues that could be potentially divisive between you and another believer who holds a different view on the same issue. Do you think you experience more restriction or more freedom in this area? According to these verses, how should you respond to those who don't agree with you?

The possibilities for conflict in non-essential issues are endless. I wish I could see what you wrote down, but my list included:

- Education: public, private, homeschool, other?

- Sabbath: when, what, how?

- Bible translations: is one translation "the one"?

- Vaccines: yes, no, or maybe?

- Alcohol: to drink or not to drink?

- Political affiliation and voting responsibility: is there only one "right" answer?

These are just off the top of my head. Through the years I've seen godly Christians divide over Halloween, natural birth/epidurals, smoking, worship styles, and a myriad of other things—and all still be faithful disciples of Jesus.

> **Do these verses convict or challenge you regarding any convictions you hold? If so, what help and hope do they offer?**

Paul was not advocating we do away with our convictions. He simply commanded us to love each other more than we love our convictions. For example, let's say my Christian conviction was that I shouldn't color my hair. (I do not hold this conviction!) But I had a sister in the Lord who went from blond to purple to red in the course of a year. First of all, because of my conviction, it would be wrong for me to color my hair. At the same time, my friend, who felt the freedom to color her hair, would be right to do so. So even though we differ in our convictions, because we love each other, we choose to not bully, judge, persuade, or despise each other! This is how Paul commanded us to handle diversity of conviction.

> **Look back at Romans 12:3-5. How do these verses remind you of the posture you should take toward your brothers and sisters in Christ? Write down the name of one person whom you struggle to love due to differing convictions. Pray for him/her, yourself, and your relationship.**

Paul continued this conversation in the verses we will look at tomorrow and even into Day One of Session Nine. Apparently, division between believers was as prevalent in the Roman church as it can be in ours. But, as Paul argued, if we as Christians are truly living in view of God's mercies, how can we not also extend mercy to all our brothers and sisters in Christ?

DIGGING DEEPER
Check out these verses to help you better understand today's passage:
Psalm 133 • Galatians 5:13-23 • Colossians 2:16-23

DAY 5

DO NOT JUDGE ONE ANOTHER

READ ROMANS 14:13-23.

Imagine four friends from church going out to enjoy dinner together. One of the four is convinced believers going into a bar would displease God. The other three believe they have the Christian freedom to go. What should the three friends do? Tease the one and pressure her into going? Try to persuade her and tell her why they think she's wrong? Go anyway and let her make the choice—join them or miss out? What should the one do? Give in to peer pressure? Go with her friends so that she doesn't stand out? What would you do in such a situation?

Paul gave us clear answers. If you are the one with the conviction not to go into the bar, then don't go into the bar! If you're one who feels the freedom to go, do not judge (v. 13), do not cause your friend to stumble (vv. 13,20), and keep your convictions to yourself (v. 22). In other words, gladly, cheerfully give up your right to go to the bar in order to love your friend.

Do you agree with this? If so, why? If not, why not?

Being right is not the chief Christian virtue. Love is. That doesn't mean you won't be in the right sometimes. You will. And it certainly doesn't mean that a correct understanding of what God loves, requires, and commands isn't important. It is! But we can take our good understanding and deep convictions and use them in sinful ways—we can cause our brothers and sisters to stumble and cause division in the body of Christ.

Read Romans 15:1-2. How did Paul let the reader know where he stood on the issue? Yet what did he command (14:13)?

Paul didn't correct the convictions of either group. He believed the strong, the ones who felt more freedom, were "right," but he didn't correct the believers with a stricter conscience. And he didn't command the stronger believers to instruct, convince, or enlighten their weaker brothers and sisters.

> **What are some ways the stronger believers in Rome could have put stumbling blocks in front of their brothers and sisters who believed eating meat was not God honoring?**

I have two good friends who have a diversity of conviction. Friend one, "Sally," is not comfortable looking at any image of Jesus—in a movie, art, or book—feeling it is a violation of the second commandment which says to not make a carved image (Ex. 20:4). Friend two, "Jane," does not share that conviction, but she does respect her friend's desire to please the Lord and her right to differ in their convictions. Sally visited Jane's house over Christmas, so Jane removed Baby Jesus from the manger in all the Nativity sets she had displayed. Not because she thought having a Baby Jesus figurine was wrong, but because she didn't want to grieve Sally. And Sally didn't judge Jane or look down on her for the freedom she had in her convictions.

> **How much diversity of conviction is there within your circle of close friends? How much diversity of conviction is there within your church? In what ways do you show love to one another in your diversity? How can you "decide never to put a stumbling block or hindrance in the way of a brother [or sister]" (Rom. 14:13)?**

We're so prone to gather with those who agree with us and form "tribes" around convictions about non-essentials. In fact, church splits and the formation of new churches have happened over this type of tribalism.

Convictions are good. Tribalism isn't. We're not called to flatten our differences. We're called to lay down our rights. In fact, laying down our rights is one of the most Christ-like things we can do. Paul wrote in Philippians 2:5-8:

> Have this mind among yourselves, which is yours in Christ Jesus, who, though he was in the form of God, did not count equality with God a thing to be grasped, but emptied himself, by taking the form of a servant, being born in the likeness of men. And being found in human form, he humbled himself by becoming obedient to the point of death, even death on a cross.

This is how we are to love one another. Take the form of a servant, humble yourself, and be willing to sacrifice your rights. This is the mind and the way of Christ.

According to Romans 14:17, what are the characteristics of the kingdom of God?

Why do you think Paul reminded his readers of those characteristics at this point in the letter?

What does verse 18 indicate about who we're really serving when we serve others in this way?

What was Paul's conclusion in verse 19?

Verse 20 is a warning about what can happen if we don't pursue the characteristics of the kingdom. How can the work of God be destroyed "for the sake of food" (v. 20)?

In reality, we've probably all fallen on both sides of the weak-strong continuum. For most of us, our consciences convict us in one area, but in another we feel more freedom. As we grow in the Lord and our knowledge of what pleases Him, some of our convictions change. This should give us empathy for others as well as remind us to treat others like we want to be treated.

Both the strong and the weak sister have to be aware of the "pitfalls" of her position. The stronger believer, the one with more freedom, has to be careful that her freedom doesn't turn into antinomianism or license to sin. And the more restricted believer has to be careful her convictions don't turn into legalism and marks of righteousness. (If you've forgotten what these phrases mean, turn back to Session Five, Day Three on p. 97.) Our only righteousness is Jesus.

> Review the verses from yesterday and today (Rom. 14:1-23) and write two to three ways the stronger believer should live and two to three ways the weaker believer should live.

> What is one action step these verses have compelled you to take?

I will repeat what I said at the beginning of Day Four. If we, in the body of Christ, would understand and obey what Paul has told us in these verses, I am convinced our churches, our witness, and our walks with the Lord would grow. Sister, let us together pursue what makes for peace and mutual upbuilding that the work of God would not be destroyed (Rom. 14:20) but that His kingdom of righteousness would grow—for our good and His glory.

DIGGING DEEPER
Check out these verses to help you better understand today's passage:
1 Corinthians 10:23-24 • 1 Corinthians 10:31-33 • Philippians 2:1-4

Session Eight: UNDERSTANDING THE BATTLE

WATCH Session Eight video teaching.

1. In view of God's mercies

_____

_____

_____

_____

_____

_____

2. Present your bodies

_____

_____

_____

_____

_____

_____

3. Be transformed

_____

_____

_____

_____

_____

_____

VIDEO & GROUP GUIDE

DISCUSSION QUESTIONS

1   What day of personal study had the most impact on you? Why?

2   How did what you heard on the video teaching clarify, reinforce, or give new insight to what you studied this session?

3   Why is Paul's comparison of the church to a body such a great illustration? How integral do you view your part in the body of your local church?

4   In what ways is submission to authority a way for Christians to love their neighbor?

5   What is one non-essential issue that could be potentially divisive between you and someone who holds a different view on the same issue? How were you encouraged to love that person this week?

6   What new mercies did you see in the passage this session?

7   What is the most significant thing you learned about God, the gospel, or yourself this session?

To access the video teaching sessions, use the instructions in the back of your Bible study book.

SESSION EIGHT   187

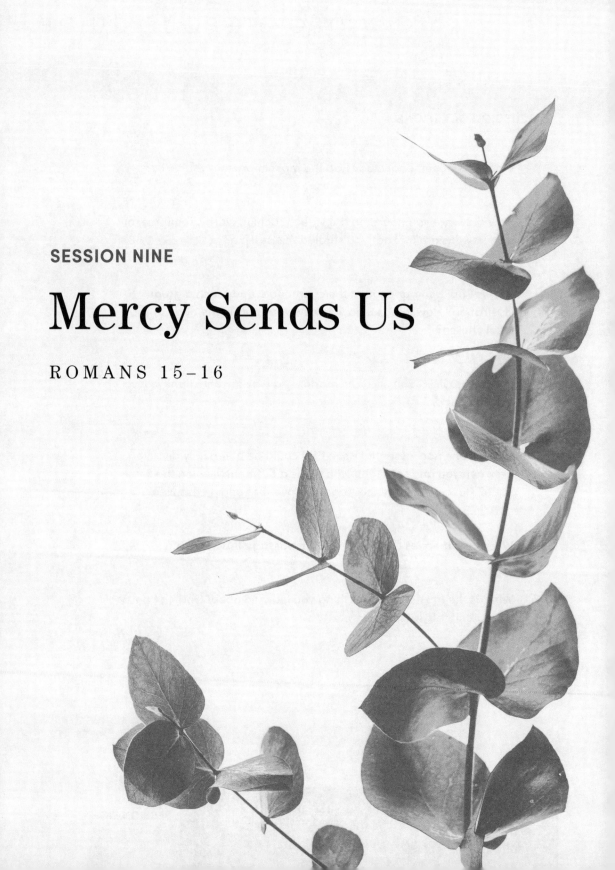

SESSION NINE

Mercy Sends Us

ROMANS 15–16

Introduction

I have a friend who is passionate about sharing any and all of her great discoveries. If she finds a hair product that makes her hair shiny, she buys a few extra for her friends to try. When she discovers a cleaning technique that simplifies her life, she posts all over social media. A new superfood, type of exercise, or energy drink becomes the topic of many conversations. Basically, when she discovers good news, she cannot keep it to herself.

I think Paul would have loved my friend. He knew that good news has to be shared. His goal throughout the letter to the church in Rome was to reveal the need for the gospel (1:18–3:20), unveil the power and beauty of the gospel (3:21–11), show his readers how the gospel transforms lives (12–14), and then compel believers to share the gospel with others (15–16).

Many of us want to stop with understanding the gospel. We like knowledge and can confuse increased understanding with spiritual maturity. Others are tempted to stop with their own transformation and sanctification. But, as important as those are, they're not the end game. In fact, I would argue that we haven't really understood or been transformed by the gospel if we aren't increasingly compelled and equipped to tell others about the salvation we have received.

As Paul wrapped up his letter to his brothers and sisters in Rome, he reminded his readers—then and now—to love each other deeply, let that love be a visible demonstration of the grace they have received, and participate in the proclamation of the gospel of that grace to all the world.

MEMORY VERSES

> Now to him who is able to strengthen you according to my gospel and the preaching of Jesus Christ, according to the revelation of the mystery that was kept secret for long ages but has now been disclosed and through the prophetic writings has been made known to all nations, according to the command of the eternal God, to bring about the obedience of faith—to the only wise God be glory forevermore through Jesus Christ! Amen.

ROMANS 16:25-27

Prayer for the Week

Father, You are so good to me. Your mercy, love, forgiveness, and kindness overwhelm me. Thank You for the goodness of the gospel—that I can be given the perfect righteousness of Your Son. Meet with me, by Your Spirit, in Your Word, as I study the last two chapters in Romans. Continue to transform me and conform me into the image of Jesus. Would You open new doors for me to tell others about Jesus and then give me the boldness and winsomeness I need to do so? Help me never to be ashamed of, but to boldly proclaim to others, the great salvation that is mine in You. I ask this in the glorious name of Jesus, **Amen.**

SERVE BY WELCOMING

READ ROMANS 15:1-13.

Have you ever noticed that maintaining unity is hard while creating disunity is easy? Disunity happens naturally when we simply stop trying. Healthy relationships—friendships, marriage, parents/children, with our brothers and sisters in Christ—take work. In the same way that my house will become dirtier and messier (not cleaner and more organized) if left untended, our relationships will weaken, dissolve, or devolve if neglected. But when we apply intentionality and effort toward our relationships, they can thrive. Paul wanted his readers to see that unity in the body of Christ takes work, but the work is well worth the effort because our unity brings glory to God.

In verse 2, Paul talked about how we treat our "neighbor." Most of us picture a next-door neighbor when we hear this word. But when Jesus taught the parable of the good Samaritan (Luke 10:25-37), He showed us that our neighbors include not only the people who live around us, but also our coworkers, family members, people in our communities—really anyone the Lord puts in our path. In these verses, however, Paul was speaking specifically about our relationships within our local church.

Paul told us in the first two verses to bear with one another, not please ourselves, work to please our neighbors, and build them up. In the chart, write down what those phrases mean, followed by listing at least one way you can carry out each instruction.

	What does it mean?	What can I do?
Bear with the failings of others.		
Don't seek to please yourself.		
Seek to please your neighbor.		
Build her up.		

These are remarkably simple exhortations. In theory. In practice they are extremely diffi-cult to do. Impatience and selfishness make it hard to bear with others. We want to have our way and get frustrated with those who get in our way. In the church, bickering and fights break out because we seek to please ourselves in issues like style of worship, kind of music, type of youth group, color of paint, and whether to have pews or chairs. When we seek to please ourselves, get our own way, and build ourselves up, we are doing the opposite of what Paul commanded.

To live out the simple but hard exhortations means we have to put effort and intentionality behind it. We don't naturally gravitate toward pleasing others. Thankfully, Paul wasn't like the clothing brand Nike®—he didn't tell us to "Just do it." Instead, he rooted his instruc-tions in what Jesus has done for us.

> **How does the truth of Romans 15:3 (which is the understatement of all time) help you in your pursuit of unity?**

In verses 4-6, Paul not only gave the example of Christ, he showed the necessity of time in the Word and prayer. Sometimes we think unity is something we can achieve in our own strength, but true unity requires the power of God. Yes, we participate. We have to intentionally lay down our rights, seek the good of others, bear with them in patience, and build others up. But we are unable to do those things without the transformative power of the Word and the enabling power of prayer.

> **In verse 4, what two things do we receive from the Scripture, and what is the result? In what ways have you received each of these through God's Word?**

> **What did Paul pray for in verses 5-6? How did he incorporate what he said in verse 4?**

> **What was his ultimate request for his readers?**

How have you seen (or how would you like to see) Paul's prayer answered in your church?

The theme song from the '80s sitcom *Cheers* regularly runs through my head. The chorus highlights how we want to go to the place where everyone knows us and is always glad to see us.

The underlying message is that everybody is looking to belong, to be known, and accepted. Everyone. The writers of *Cheers* presumed that the neighborhood bar was as good a place as any to find this acceptance. But the church should provide the best welcome of all. We should be the place where others can say, "They knew my name. They were always glad I came." Why? Because Jesus has done that for us.

Read verse 7. How has Jesus welcomed you?

How can you do the same for others?

List as many practical ways as you can come up with for providing a true welcome to:

• Guests to your church on a Sunday morning:

• Your literal neighbor:

• Your spouse or family member:

• A coworker or new friend:

Do you remember where the church in Rome suffered the greatest division? It was between the Jewish and the Gentile believers. The Jewish Christians struggled to believe that the Gentile Christians had been fully brought into the faith since they had not been given the Law. So Paul took his readers back to the Old Testament to show them that God's plan had always been to create a diverse, multi-ethnic, but gloriously unified church.

Read the four Old Testament quotations (vv. 9,10,11,12). What will the ultimate result be (v. 9)?

A repeated refrain throughout Scripture is, "I will be your God, and you will be my people" (Ex. 6:7; Lev. 26:12; Jer. 32:38; Ezek. 36:28; Rev. 21:3). God is creating a people for Himself in Christ, and this one people of God will come from every tribe, tongue, nation, and people group. The unity of this diverse group of people—every language singing in one voice, every nation and tribe under one King—will bring praise and glory to God. And it will be our unity that proclaims the validity of our gospel. Does our unity matter? Yes, with eternal ramifications!

> In Romans 15:12–13, the word *hope* is used three times. Where is our hope anchored? How do we abound in hope?

In this passage, Paul only used the plural form of the word for *you*.[1] Depending on where you're from, you might want to read that *you* as *you all* or *y'all*. But the point is that we are to read these verses with other believers in mind.

- Verse 5: May God grant y'all endurance and encouragement to live in harmony,

- Verse 6: so that with one voice all of you can glorify God.

- Verse 7: Welcome one another as Christ has welcomed you all.

- Verse 13: May the God of hope fill y'all with joy and peace so that you all may abound in hope by the power of the Holy Spirit.

As you work on your memory verses today, ask God to give you a greater love for and deeper unity with your brothers and sisters in Christ. Welcome each other with open arms and in new ways this week because you have been unreservedly welcomed by Christ Himself.

DIGGING DEEPER
Check out these verses to help you better understand today's passage:
John 17:20-23 • Philippians 2:1-7 • 3 John 9-11

SERVE BY PROCLAIMING

READ ROMANS 15:14-21.

What is my purpose in life? Why am I here?

Most of us have asked those questions at one point or another along the way. In our passage for today, Paul gave us his answer—which should also be our answer. He allowed us to see his heart and, in doing so, lifted our eyes from the immediate concerns and mundane details that can occupy our minds. He showed that our ultimate purpose, our greatest identity, is, like his, completely wrapped up in and tied to the purposes and passions of God.

God is passionate about the worldwide proclamation of the gospel. His sights have always been set on the whole world (Gen. 1:28; Gen 12:3; Ex. 19:5-6). His plan, from the beginning, was to create a people for Himself that included every tribe, nation, tongue, and people group. In other words, our God is a missional God. He is the One who seeks and saves. He is the One who goes to the lost. He is both the One who sends and the One who was sent. (The New Testament refers to Jesus as the "sent" One numerous times.) Then Jesus said in John 17 that in the same way the Father has sent Him into the world, He sends us.

That's our purpose. That's why we are here. We've been sent by Jesus to join Him on His mission to proclaim the gospel in all the world. In Christ, we have been united, not just to His righteousness, but to His heart, His passion, and His mission. It's our greatest calling and our ultimate purpose.

Review Romans 15:14-21. List four to five things you learn about Paul's passion for the proclamation of the gospel.

Depending on the translation you're using, Paul talked about his pride/boasting (v. 17), his accomplishments (v. 18), and his ambition (v. 20). Those don't sound like very godly things to mention. But Paul showed us that godly pride, godly ambition, and godly accomplishments are good things—framed in the proper context. His pride was in what God had done. His accomplishments were what Christ had done through him. And his ambition was to preach the gospel.

What is one thing you'd boast about?

What is your greatest accomplishment?

What is your greatest ambition?

How do these three things line up with Paul's?

According to verse 18:

- What dominated the content of Paul's speech? What dominates the content of your speech?

- What two means of "speech" did Paul employ?

- What do each of those mean?

Word and deed. You've probably heard the saying, "If you're going to talk the talk, you better walk the walk." Or as the grandmother of a friend of mine would ask, "Does your do match your say?" The point is, we proclaim the gospel both by what we say and by what we do.

Most of us fall to one side or the other. Some are more inclined to talk the talk, but their walks are missing the genuine love for others that would make their talk believable. Others want to just walk the walk, and the talk never happens—the content of the gospel is never shared. It takes both! We have to proclaim the gospel message—by using words like Jesus, sin, forgiveness, righteousness, and salvation—as well as live lives that show forth the fruit of a saved person—someone who loves mercy, seeks justice, walks humbly, shows compassion, and demonstrates kindness. Word and deed.

Do you gravitate more toward word or deed, talk or walk? In what ways are you challenged to incorporate both?

What needs to happen for you to take steps toward both?

Like Paul, this is how we participate in God's mission. Did you see how Paul proclaimed the gospel both organically and strategically? Organically by telling people about Jesus wherever he was. Strategically by making plans to go to new places for the purpose of telling people about Jesus. We are to do the same. This is how we fulfill our purpose, by living on purpose—sharing about Jesus both where we are and where we might go.

Think through the relational spheres you move about in. Are you in a book or dinner club? Do you drive carpool? Do you have a group of people you exercise with? Coworkers? Fellow board members? Do you meet people when you travel? Do you work for someone, or does someone work for you?

Why do you think the Lord has placed you in each sphere? How can you live on purpose in each of those relationships?

Is God bringing any specific person to mind right now? If so, what steps can you take this week to share the gospel with him or her? If not, ask God to open your eyes and heart to see those in your spheres of life that need Christ.

Who is the last person you told about salvation in Jesus? Is there someone in your spheres of life that you can tell this week?

Paul not only preached the gospel wherever he was, he also desired to preach the gospel in places where Jesus was not yet known. This truth is astounding to me—there are still people in the world who have literally never heard the name of Jesus. Never. They have no idea that the Son of God was born, lived the life we could never live, and died the death we deserve. They have never heard that this man, Jesus, rose from the dead and is able to save our souls! As Paul wrote in Romans 10, "How then will they call on him in whom they have not believed? And how are they to believe in him of whom they have never heard? And how are they to hear without someone preaching? And how are they to preach unless they are sent?" (vv. 14-15).

My hope is that God is working in all of our lives as we study Romans—saving, transforming, sanctifying, and compelling us all to live our lives on purpose. I pray that God is conforming us more into the image of His Son, making us unashamed of the gospel, and equipping us to share it with people all around us. And I am praying that He will use His Word to call some of us to go to places where the name of Jesus has not been heard.

How is your study of Romans changing you? In what ways are you being transformed? In what ways are you being compelled to live on purpose?

I'll say it again; our God is a missional God. He is on a global and eternal mission to seek and save the lost. His passion is to be our God, for us to be His people, and to dwell with us forever. What honor He bestows on us when He invites us to join Him. Will you?

DIGGING DEEPER
Check out these verses to help you better understand today's passage:
Matthew 28:18-20 • 1 Corinthians 3:5-9 • 2 Corinthians 10:13-18

DAY 3

SERVE BY PARTNERING

READ ROMANS 15:22-33.

Do you remember when Paul wrote his letter to the church in Rome? Or where he was when he wrote it? Or what he was doing? Feel free to go back to page 16 and refresh your memory! In a nutshell, in AD 57, Paul was in the city of Corinth on his third missionary journey. He hadn't been to Rome yet but was very eager to go.

Read verses 22-28 and describe Paul's travel plans. Where was he planning to go, and what was he planning to do in each place? (Look back to your map on p. 16.)

First, he planned to leave Corinth and go to Jerusalem.

> What did the Christians in Macedonia and Achaia (modern day Greece) do for the churches in Jerusalem?

> Do you think the churches in Macedonia and Achaia were made up of predominantly Jewish or Gentile believers?

> What was their attitude toward their action?

> How do you think this attitude displayed and promoted unity in the church?

> Based on what you have learned in Romans, why do you think Paul wrote, "they owe it to them" (v. 27)?

The churches in Macedonia and Achaia, made up mainly of Gentile believers, understood they owed a debt of gratitude to those through whom the gospel had come to them—and they were glad to give. They also understood the interconnectedness of the global church. Their gift to the church in Jerusalem displayed and promoted unity among believers across ethnic, national, socio-economic, and cultural lines. No wonder Paul was eager to take their gift to Jerusalem!

But we know something Paul didn't know at the time he wrote the letter. Though he did eventually travel from Jerusalem to Rome, the journey wasn't as he expected—because things in Jerusalem didn't go exactly as he had hoped.

When you have time, read Acts 21–28 to get the full story. But here's what transpired in a nutshell: Paul went to Jerusalem and the offering we read about was accepted. But then Paul was arrested by the Jewish leaders and spent two years in a Jerusalem prison. After a series of trials, Paul was sent to Rome, in chains, to be placed under house arrest while he waited for a trial before Caesar. This was when he would have first met the believers he was writing to in the letter we're studying. His journey to Rome was fraught with all the drama and adventure of any blockbuster movie—but don't take my word for it; read Acts 27!

Eventually, probably between AD 64–67, Paul was beheaded as a martyr in Rome. Whether or not Paul reached Spain before he died remains a mystery. There is some evidence to suggest he did, but we will have to wait and ask him in person in the new heavens and new earth. What great conversations we will have!

Knowing that Paul's well-thought-out strategy didn't exactly go as he hoped should influence how we plan, our need to rest in God's providence, and how we pray. Obviously, Paul hoped to proclaim the gospel to the ends of the earth, and he had clear plans to accomplish it. But he also knew that "the heart of man plans his way, but the LORD establishes his steps" (Prov. 16:9).

In Romans 15:30-32, what three things did Paul ask them to pray?

What do you learn about how to pray for others from these verses?

What do you think it means to strive in prayer?

How does knowing about Paul's difficulties in Jerusalem highlight the importance of the phrase "by God's will" (v. 32)?

What plans are you currently making? How should the instructions in these verses, and particularly the phrase "by God's will," influence how you plan, pray, and trust God's providence?

How long had Paul been wanting to go to Rome? He invited the believers in Rome to partner with him in his plans to go to Spain in what two ways (vv. 24,30)?

Worldwide gospel proclamation requires the participation of the full body of Christ. Some need to go. Some need to give. Everyone needs to pray. We see all of those ways present in this passage. Paul was eager to go to Spain. He asked the church in Rome to help and to pray. Two things worth noting: *helping* means to support financially as well as in other ways, and *praying* is active work.

What opportunities—going, giving, sending, praying—do you have to partner with others in the spread of the gospel? How are you currently participating?

Financial giving is always necessary for the spread of the gospel. Today, the people going need plane tickets, insurance, food, clothes, housing—they have to live! But there are so many other ways to give. Some churches need to send leaders and congregants in order to start a new church in a place that lacks a gospel presence. Some churches invest in a person's theological education only to send that person across town or across the ocean. Families might have to give up the hope of living in the same town in order to send children or siblings to proclaim the gospel. Giving comes in many shapes and sizes.

We are all called to give in some way. What might you be called to give? Is your attitude about giving the same as the churches in Macedonia and Achaia who were "pleased to do it" (v. 27)?

Paul had a plan. He was passionate about the proclamation of the gospel. He asked others to participate with him by striving in prayer and joyfully giving. Do you have a plan? Consider the relational spheres we thought about yesterday. Pray for open doors in those friendships. Strive in prayer for the gospel to go out. Come up with a plan for giving, going, sending, and praying.

What can you pray? What can you give? Where can you go?

One of the great purposes of our lives is to participate in the proclamation of the gospel. Let's strive in prayer for each other in this. Let's give generously so those going can go. And may the Lord send some of us doing this study to the ends of the earth in service to Him.

DIGGING DEEPER
Check out these verses to help you better understand today's passage:
Psalm 22:27 • 2 Corinthians 8:1-5 • Colossians 4:2-4

SERVE WITH OTHERS

READ ROMANS 16:1-23.

My favorite part of the Academy Awards is the acceptance speeches. I love hearing the names of everyone who has helped and influenced the person winning the award. The award winners acknowledge they haven't achieved the honor on their own and are grateful for everyone who participated with them along the way.

Romans 16 functions in a similar way. Paul demonstrated his gratitude for many who were laboring in gospel ministry in Rome. Although you might be tempted to skip over this list of names, understand that Romans 16 does more than simply offer thanks—it reveals what life in the church is meant to be.

In verses 1-15, Paul mentioned twenty-five people by name, two family groups (those "who belong to the family of . . ."), and two by their relationship to someone in the list (i.e. mother or sister of someone). Try to find them all and list them in the chart below and on the next page. In the other two columns, write what Paul said about that person relationally and/or what he said about that person's work. (Note: There are some people who are only mentioned by name. Nothing is said about their relationship to Paul or their work.)

Name	Relationship	Ministry Work

Name	Relationship	Ministry Work

Everyone listed in verses 1-15 was in Rome with the exception of Phoebe (v. 1)—who is described as a servant of the church in Cenchreae. Cenchreae was the eastern harbor on the Corinthian isthmus, about five miles from Corinth, so it's widely believed she is the one who carried this letter from Paul to the church in Rome.[2] Paul had not been to Rome, yet he knew these people either because they had crossed paths with him in other locations or he had heard of their work in the Lord.

As you look at the list, what stands out to you?

One thing I notice in this list is the number of people needed to accomplish the work. These were not "professional" or paid ministry leaders. We can assume they were funding, hosting, instructing, showing mercy, going, sending, and giving practical care and help. The work of the church was accomplished by the people in the church.

It is very common for people today to think that the work of ministry should be done by the "professionals"—paid pastors and ministry leaders. But that has never been the case. In the video teaching for Session Two, we saw in Ephesians how Paul clarified the work of ministry leaders is "to equip the saints [people in the church] for the work of ministry" (Eph. 4:12).

What is your understanding of how the work of gospel ministry is to be done? What do you see as your role in this ministry?

Another striking feature of the list is the great diversity of people: men and women, Jew and Gentile, rich and poor, slave and free. This list exemplifies what Paul wrote about the church in Galatians 3:28—that "there is neither Jew nor Greek, there is neither slave nor free, there is no male and female, for you are all one in Christ Jesus."

Ten of the people mentioned are women—Phoebe, Prisca, Mary, Junia, Tryphaena, Tryphosa, Persis, Rufus's mother, Julia, and Nereus's sister. Most scholars agree that Ampliatus, Urbanus, Hermes, Philologus, and Julia "were common names for slaves."[3] The two family groups mentioned, Narcissus and Aristobulus, were most likely prominent, wealthy, and powerful families in Rome. And they all—men, women, rich, poor, the powerful, and the powerless— labored side by side in gospel ministry in the local church.

> Think about the dynamics of this group for a minute. What effect do you think their love for each other and their unity of purpose might have had on unbelievers in Rome?

In what ways would their diversity have strengthened the church?

In what ways might it have been a challenge?

A CLOSER LOOK
"The God of peace will soon crush Satan under your feet" (Rom. 16:20). Through His death and resurrection, Jesus crushed the head of the serpent and fulfilled Genesis 3:15. We now live between the time when Jesus defeated Satan and the time when Jesus will come again and completely annihilate him (Rev. 20:10). During this in-between time, it's the church, as the body of Christ, who continually crushes Satan under our feet with every spiritual victory we experience by God's grace.

A CLOSER LOOK
"Greet one another with a holy kiss" (Rom. 16:16). The cultural greeting in Paul's day (as is still true in many parts of the world) was to offer a kiss on the cheek. This was a greeting between friends and not sexual or sensual in any way. Today we offer the same type of warm, affectionate greetings to our friends with a hearty handshake or a friendly hug. Paul's point is that we should warmly greet our fellow brothers and sisters in Christ with platonic but genuine affection.

How diverse is the group of people you worship and partner with in gospel ministry?

We've noted throughout the study that the Jew/Gentile makeup of the church seemed to be a challenge to their unity. But in verses 17-20, Paul called out a specific group that threatened to wreak havoc in the church: false teachers. It's important to note that after spending all of chapter fourteen and part of chapter fifteen exhorting the believers in Rome to bear with each other, welcome the weaker ones, not to pass judgment on each other, and accept one another, Paul adamantly commanded them to watch out for and avoid false teachers.

Why the sharp distinction? Why would Paul tell them to bear with some and watch out for others? Because doctrine matters. We are to bear with each other over disputable matters, but not over essential doctrine. The content of the gospel matters!

How has this study of Romans helped grow your understanding of the gospel of grace and the importance of guarding it?

A CLOSER LOOK
Tertius served as Paul's scribe which means he wrote down what Paul said.

In Romans 16:21-23, Paul mentioned eight people who were with him in Corinth. List their names and anything about them you find interesting.

The spread of the gospel, one of our greatest purposes, requires all-hands-on-deck. You, like the people Paul mentioned, have been given gifts that the church needs. You have a unique part to play in the redemption of all things. You are needed.

Keeping in mind how all the people Paul mentioned in Romans 16:1-23 were vital parts of the ministry of the gospel, reflect on and respond to the questions in the following chart:

Questions to ponder	Response
How connected are you to your local church?	
How invested are you in the work of ministry?	
What hinders you from serving?	
How deeply do you know and love the people in your church?	
What gifts do you have, and how can you use them in ministry service?	

The great apostle Paul was dependent on and connected with believers all over the known world. He knew that the spread of the gospel required a diversity of people, doing a variety of work. He delighted in his co-laborers, knew them by name, affirmed their work, and rejoiced in their partnership. That is what life in a healthy church looks like.

DIGGING DEEPER
Check out these verses to help you better understand today's passage:
Mark 15:21 • John 1–4 • Acts 18:24-26

SERVE FOR GOD'S GLORY

READ ROMANS 16:25-27.

Oh, friend, we're here. We've arrived at the end of this magnificent letter. What a privilege it has been to go on this journey with you. And what glories we have seen! We've peered at the depths of God's grace, the heights of His mercy, and the breadth of His love to save us. As we wrap up, how should we respond to all we have seen and learned? The same way Paul did—with **PRAISE**, adoration, and worship.

DOXOLOGY
The offering of praise to God (see Rom. 11:33-36; 16:25-27).

BENEDICTION
The giving of a blessing (see Rom. 15:13; 15:33).

Paul began his letter to the Romans with the gospel (1:1) and he now ends with the gospel. In Session Two, Day Three (p. 23), you were asked to write down your understanding of the gospel. Go back, read what you wrote, and then comment here on anything you would add or alter. In other words, how has your understanding of the gospel—what it is and what it does—changed?

In verses 25-26, Paul said "according to the revelation of the mystery that was kept secret for long ages but has now been disclosed." What was the mystery, and how has it been revealed or disclosed? (See Rom. 1:16-17 and 3:21-22 to remind yourself.)

Paul wrote that God is able to strengthen you according to the "gospel and the preaching of Jesus Christ" (Rom. 16:25). Some translations say, "establish you" or "make you strong." How do you think this happens?

Are there areas in your life where you feel fragile, frail, ungrounded, unstable, tired, and/or timid? Explain.

How can God strengthen and establish you through the gospel and the preaching of Jesus Christ this week?

Our God has the power to save, the power to keep, the power to transform, and the power to strengthen. The power of God that rescued you is the power of God that sustains you. The gospel that saved you is the same gospel that keeps you. When you are weak and weary, run to His gospel of grace found in His Word and be strengthened by His power.

According to verse 26, to whom has this gospel been disclosed? For what purpose?

Go back to Romans 1:5. What similarities do you see?

What do you learn about the mission of God in this verse?

What do you learn about the importance of the obedience that is a result of true faith?

The main point of Paul's final verse in this glorious book was an appropriate one to end with—the wisdom and glory of God.

How have you seen the wisdom of God in Romans? How have you seen the wisdom of God in your own life?

We began our journey together by acknowledging both the ordinary and the extraordinary ways God works through His living Word. As we continue to seek Him, He works in us to change us, transform, renew, establish, rebuke, instruct, and conform us more and more to the image of Jesus.

How has God met you in this study?

How are you more conformed to the image of His Son?

How are you more captivated by His mission to seek and save the lost because of your time in Romans?

In the ESV translation, the last seven words of Romans are "be glory forevermore through Jesus Christ! Amen." Glory. Forever. Because of Jesus. Amen. Paul was astounded at all God had done to plan and accomplish our salvation. The praise that burst forth from his heart happened as he thought again about the mercies of God. The salvation that rests entirely on God's grace is rooted completely in God's mercy—and should always result in God's praise.

Considering all you've learned and experienced in this study of Romans, write your own doxology in the space provided.

What a joy it has been to study this letter with you! I look forward to the day we will be face-to-face, either in this life or in glory, and can share our delight as we worship and praise God together. Until then, let me leave you with my own benediction.

May the God of our salvation establish you firmly in the righteousness of the Son. May the Spirit strengthen you and remind you of the deep love of the Father. And, in view of God's abundant mercies, may the gift of the gospel transform you more into the image of the Son and send you into all the world with the good news that His great mercy is available for all.

DIGGING DEEPER
Check out these verses to help you better understand today's passage:
Philippians 1:6 • 1 Timothy 1:17 • Jude 24-25

Session Nine: THE MISSION

WATCH Session Nine video teaching.

1. Where do I go?

_____

_____

_____

_____

_____

_____

_____

2. What do I do?

_____

_____

_____

_____

_____

_____

_____

DISCUSSION QUESTIONS

1 What day of personal study had the most impact on you? Why?

2 How did what you heard on the video teaching clarify, reinforce, or give new insight to what you studied this session?

3 How has Jesus welcomed you? How can you do the same for others?

4 How do you participate in the worldwide proclamation of the gospel?

5 How have you seen the wisdom of God in Romans? How have you seen the wisdom of God in your own life?

6 What new mercies did you see in the passage this session?

7 What is the most significant thing you learned about God, the gospel, or yourself this session?

To access the video teaching sessions, use the instructions in the back of your Bible study book.

Leader Guide

A WORD TO THE LEADER

Thanks for taking on the responsibility of leading your group through *In View of God's Mercies*! What a blessing you will experience as you lead women through this study on Romans. Here are some tips to help you effectively lead the study.

FORMAT OF THE STUDY

1. GROUP SESSIONS

Each group session contains the following elements:

GATHER: This is a time to greet and welcome everyone. In the first session, we've provided some questions to introduce the study and help get the discussion going. In the subsequent sessions, we've provided one to two opening questions for the group to consider. These are intended to be quick-answer questions to set the stage for what will be discussed in your group time.

WATCH: Each week you'll show a video teaching. You'll find detailed information on how to access the videos on the card inserted in the back of the Bible study book. If your group doesn't have adequate Internet connection for video streaming, DVD sets are available for purchase at lifeway.com/mercies.

Encourage participants to take notes from the video teaching on the WATCH pages in their Bible study books.

DISCUSS: Following the video, you'll lead a time of discussion to help your group debrief both the previous session of personal study and what they heard on the video teaching. We've provided a list of questions on the Group Time pages to help foster this discussion. Feel free to adapt, skip, or add questions according to the needs of your group.

CLOSE: We've provided you a brief idea on how to close each session, but be sensitive to the Holy Spirit's direction. This study is filled with much discussion about the gospel and will surely lead to moments and opportunities for your group members to know Christ for the first time or more intimately. Each week make sure to leave time for the women to say their memory verse(s) out loud. This should be fun (not anxiety-inducing!) and encourage the women in the habit of memorizing Scripture.

2. PERSONAL STUDY

Each session contains five days of personal study to help participants dig into God's Word for themselves. Encourage and challenge participants to complete each day of study while also giving grace to those who may struggle to do so.

PREPARE

Take time each week to personally prepare to lead your group.

STUDY: Make sure you've watched the video teaching and completed each session's personal study before the group session. Review the discussion questions and consider how best to lead your group through this time.

PRAY: Set aside time each week to pray for yourself and each member of your group.

CONNECT: Find ways to interact and stay engaged with each member of your group throughout the study. Make use of social media, email, and handwritten notes to encourage them.

SESSION ONE

GATHER: Welcome participants to the study and distribute Bible study books to each group member. Encourage discussion by asking the following questions:

- What drew you to this study?

- What were your thoughts when you first heard the title of this study: *In View of God's Mercies*?

- How familiar are you with the book of Romans? Explain.

- When you hear the word *gospel*, what do you think?

- What do you hope to get out of this study?

WATCH: Play the video teaching for Session One. Encourage participants to take notes or jot down questions on the WATCH page (p. 9).

DISCUSS: Use the questions found on page 9 to debrief the video teaching.

CLOSE: Divide participants into groups of three to four and provide time for them to share prayer requests with each other about their hopes for this study. Encourage one member of each small group to lead their group in a closing prayer if they're comfortable doing so.

SESSION TWO

GATHER: Welcome participants back to the study. Use the following question to set the stage for what will be discussed in your group time:

- When was the last time you wrote a letter, and to whom did you write it?

- If you were writing a letter to some friends who were new Christians, what would be some things you'd want to say to them about following Christ?

WATCH: Play the video teaching for Session Two. Encourage participants to take notes or jot down questions on the WATCH page (p. 32).

DISCUSS: Use the questions found on page 33 to debrief the previous session of personal study and the video teaching.

CLOSE: Provide time for group members to assess if they have conflict or broken relationships with anyone in the body of Christ. Encourage them to consider how the gospel unites them and gives them common ground to reconcile their differences. Lead your group in prayer, thanking God for the gospel and praying for those who need to mend relationships. Don't forget to allow time for the women to practice their memory verses.

SESSION THREE

GATHER: Welcome participants back to the study. Use the following questions to set the stage for what will be discussed in your group time:

- What's the "best" (most outlandish, most unbelievable . . .) excuse you've ever heard?

- Are you more likely to take medicine you don't need or refuse to take medicine you do need? Explain.

WATCH: Play the video teaching for Session Three. Encourage participants to take notes or jot down questions on the WATCH page (p. 58).

DISCUSS: Use the questions found on page 59 to debrief the previous session of personal study and the video teaching.

CLOSE: Provide a moment for group members to consider the seriousness of sin and how it has affected their lives and the lives of those around them. Lead them to pray for those around them who are trapped in sin and need to be rescued through the power of Christ. Allow time for the women to practice their memory verse.

SESSION FOUR

GATHER: Welcome participants back to the study. Use the following questions to set the stage for what will be discussed in your group time:

- Have you ever served on a jury? If so, share briefly about your experience.

- What was the last thing you boasted about (even just to yourself)?

WATCH: Play the video teaching for Session Four. Encourage participants to take notes or jot down questions on the WATCH page (p. 84).

DISCUSS: Use the questions found on page 85 to debrief the previous session of personal study and the video teaching.

CLOSE: Provide a brief time for a few group members to share their "But now . . . In Christ" testimonies—where they were before they knew Christ and how He has changed their lives. Allow time for the women to practice their memory verses. Close with prayer, thanking God for His transforming work in all of your lives.

SESSION FIVE

GATHER: Welcome participants back to the study. Use the following questions to set the stage for what will be discussed in your group time:

- Have you ever bought something because of what you saw on an infomercial? If so, did it come with any "extras"?

- Can you think of a time when you were told not to do something and it made you want to do it even more? Explain.

WATCH: Play the video teaching for Session Five. Encourage participants to take notes or jot down questions on the WATCH page (p. 110).

DISCUSS: Use the questions found on page 111 to debrief the previous session of personal study and the video teaching.

CLOSE: Encourage a few group members to share what type of sin they struggle with the most. Remind them they don't have to share lots of details. It might help others to be transparent if you go first. After a time of sharing, break into smaller groups, share the memory verse, and pray for each other to be strong and live in the power of Christ.

SESSION SIX

GATHER: Welcome participants back to the study. Use the following questions to set the stage for what will be discussed in your group time:

- For those of you who like to hike, where's your favorite place to go, and what do you like best about it?

- Briefly describe a time you knew someone was interceding on your behalf.

WATCH: Play the video teaching for Session Six. Encourage participants to take notes or jot down questions on the WATCH page (p. 136).

DISCUSS: Use the questions found on page 137 to debrief the previous session of personal study and the video teaching.

CLOSE: After allowing time for the women to practice their memory verses, invite several group members to share their favorite parts of Romans 8 and why those verses are their favorites. If time allows, close with prayer, inviting group members to personalize a verse or two from Romans 8 and pray it over the group to the Father.

SESSION SEVEN

GATHER: Welcome participants back to the study. Use the following questions to set the stage for what will be discussed in your group time:

- What's the shortest trip you've ever taken?

- When you come across things that are hard to understand, are you more prone to 1) dig deeply until you find enough information to satisfy your curiosity or 2) keep moving and not worry about the details? Explain.

WATCH: Play the video teaching for Session Seven. Encourage participants to take notes or jot down questions on the WATCH page (p. 160).

DISCUSS: Use the questions found on page 161 to debrief the previous session of personal study and the video teaching.

CLOSE: After allowing time for the women to practice their memory verses, lead them to write their own doxology prayer to God using Romans 11:33–36 as a template. After a few minutes, allow several group members to read their prayers to close your time.

SESSION EIGHT

GATHER: Welcome participants back to the study. Use the following questions to set the stage for what will be discussed in your group time:

- What is one of your favorite things to watch change (i.e. seasons, children growing, friend's hair colors, styles, and so forth)?

- What is one change you have seen in yourself over the past few years?

WATCH: Play the video teaching for Session Eight. Encourage participants to take notes or jot down questions on the WATCH page (p. 186).

DISCUSS: Use the questions found on page 187 to debrief the previous session of personal study and the video teaching.

CLOSE: Provide time for some group members to share areas they are most tempted to be conformed to the world. Then ask group members to share areas of their lives where they see God transforming them into the image of Christ. Pray a prayer of thanksgiving for what God is doing in the lives of your group members. Leave time for the women to practice their memory verses.

SESSION NINE

GATHER: Welcome participants back to the study. Use the following questions to set the stage for what will be discussed in your group time

- What's the last bit of news you've shared with someone?

- When you think of the "ends of the earth," what comes to mind?

WATCH: Play the video teaching for Session Nine. Encourage participants to take notes or jot down questions on the WATCH page (p. 214).

DISCUSS: Use the questions found on page 215 to debrief the previous session of personal study and the video teaching.

CLOSE: Encourage several group members to share how they see themselves on mission for God in their everyday lives. Allow time for the women to practice their memory verses and encourage them to use the "quiz" provided at lifeway.com/mercies. Close with a time of prayer, celebrating what Christ has done in each group member through this study and praying that each member would walk out the truth they have learned.

ENDNOTES

Session Two

1. W. C. Robinson, "Apostle," ed. Geoffrey W. Bromiley, *The International Standard Bible Encyclopedia*, Revised (Wm. B. Eerdmans, 1979–1988), 192.
2. Michael Kruger, "Our Identity as God's People: Romans 1:7-15," lecture, Reformed Theological Seminary, 2014, https://rts.edu/wp-content/uploads/2014/09/Sermon-Notes-Romans-L2.pdf.
3. Strong's G40, Blue Letter Bible, accessed September 13, 2021, https://www.blueletterbible.org/lexicon/.g40/kjv/tr/0-1/.
4. The Editors of Encyclopaedia Britannica, "Gentile," *Encyclopedia Britannica*, June 3, 2021, https://www.britannica.com/topic/Gentile.
5. Christopher Ash, *Teaching Romans: Unlocking Romans 1–8 for the Bible Teacher*, eds. David Jackman and Robin Sydserff, vol. 1, Teach the Bible (Ross-shire, Scotland; London: Proclamation Trust Media; Christian Focus Publications, 2009), 55.
6. D. T. Niles, *That They May Have Life* (New York: Harper & Brothers, 1951, London: Lutterworth Press, 1962).

Session Three

1. John R. W. Stott, *The Message of Romans: God's Good News for the World*, The Bible Speaks Today (Leicester, England; Downers Grove, IL: InterVarsity Press, 2001), 69.
2. Stott, 82.
3. R. C. Sproul, *The Gospel of God: Romans* (United Kingdom: Christian Focus Publications, 2011), 51.
4. Douglas J. Moo, *Romans, The NIV Application Commentary* (Grand Rapids, MI: Zondervan Publishing House, 2000), 106.
5. Augustus Toplady, "Rock of Ages, Cleft for Me," 1776, Hymnary.org, https://hymnary.org/text/rock_of_ages_cleft_for_me_let_me_hide.

Session Four

1. Daniel Doriani, *Romans* (Phillipsburg, NJ: P & R Publishing Company, 2021).
2. Leon Morris, as quoted by John R. W. Stott in *The Message of Romans: God's Good News for the World*, The Bible Speaks Today (Leicester, England; Downers Grove, IL: InterVarsity Press, 2001), 109.
3. Bryan Chapell, RomansTalks, lecture, Reformed Presbyterian Theological Seminary, https://www.covenantseminary.edu/resources/wp-content/uploads/sites/5/2014/11/Lecture-RomansTalks-ReformedPresbyterianTheologicalSeminary-DrBryanChapell-20101211-Romans1.mp3.
4. Cornelius Plantinga Jr., *Not the Way It's Supposed to Be: A Breviary of Sin* (Grand Rapids, MI: Wm. B. Eerdmans Publishing Co., 1995), 5.
5. James Montgomery Boice and Philip Graham Ryken, *The Doctrines of Grace* (Wheaton, IL: Crossway Books, 2002), 36.
6. Benjamin Franklin, *The Autobiography of Benjamin Franklin* (Bedford, MA: Applewood Books, 2008), 139.
7. Ash, 148.
8. Doriani.
9. Karen Abbott, "The Daredevil of Niagara Falls," *Smithsonian Magazine*, October 18, 2011, https://www.smithsonianmag.com/history/the-daredevil-of-niagara-falls-110492884/.

Session Five

1. Thomas O. Chisholm, "Great Is Thy Faithfulness," 1923, Hymnary.org, https://hymnary.org/text/great_is_thy_faithfulness_o_god_my_fathe.
2. Doriani.
3. Jay Sklar, "Pentateuch," in *The T&T Clark Companion to the Doctrine of Sin*, eds. Keith L. Johnson and David Lauber (Bloomsbury: T&T Clark, 2016), 6.

4. "Question 16: What Is Sin?," The New City Catechism, https://www.thegospelcoalition.org/new-city-catechism/what-is-sin/?childrens_mode=false.

5. Merriam-Webster, s.v. "antinomian," accessed September 13, 2021, https://www.merriam-webster.com/dictionary/antinomianism.

6. Ash, 232.

7. Ibid.

8. Michael Kruger, "Objections to Justification by Faith: Can I Now Live However I Want? (Pt 3)," lecture, Reformed Theological Seminary, 2015, https://rts.edu/wp-content/uploads/2015/03/Sermon-Notes-Romans-L18.pdf.

9. Doriani.

10. "Question 12: What Does God Require in the Ninth and Tenth Commandments?," The New City Catechism, https://www.thegospelcoalition.org/new-city-catechism/what-does-god-require-in-the-ninth-and-tenth-commandments/.

11. Melissa Kruger, *Envy of Eve* (Fearn, Scotland: Christian Focus, 2012), 66.

12. John Piper, "Romans 7 Does Describe Your Christian Experience," The Gospel Coalition, January 19, 2016, https://www.thegospelcoalition.org/article/romans-7-does-describe-your-christian-experience/.

Session Six

1. John R. W. Stott, *Romans: Encountering the Gospel's Power* (United Kingdom: InterVarsity Press), 1998, 48.

2. R. C. Sproul, *Romans, St. Andrew's Expositional Commentary* (Wheaton, IL: Crossway, 2009), 251.

3. Doriani.

4. *Westminster Confession of Faith*, Chapter 12, Evangelical Presbyterian Church, by permission of Reformed Theological Seminary and Presbyterian and Reformed Publishing Company, Third Edition 2010, 15th Printing 2017, 23, https://epc.org/wp-content/uploads/Files/1-Who-We-Are/B-About-The-EPC/WCF-ModernEnglish.pdf.

5. Ash, 288.

6. "V. God's Purpose of Grace," The Baptist Faith and Message 2000, SBC, accessed October 7, 2021, https://bfm.sbc.net/bfm2000/.

7. Douglas J. Moo, *Romans, The NIV Application Commentary* (Grand Rapids, MI: Zondervan Publishing House, 2000), 280.

8. Ash, 297.

9. Ash, 298.

10. John Piper, "God Did Not Spare His Own Son," desiringGod, August 18, 2002, https://www.desiringgod.org/messages/god-did-not-spare-his-own-son.

11. Strong's G5245, Blue Letter Bible, accessed October 7, 2021, https://www.blueletterbible.org/lexicon/g5245/kjv/tr/0-1/.

12. Ash, 300.

Session Seven

1. Stephen Mansfield and David A. Holland, *Paul Harvey's America* (Chicago: Tyndale House Publishers, Inc., 2015.)

2. Christopher Ash, *Teaching Romans: Unlocking Romans 9–16 for the Bible Teacher*, eds. David Jackman and Robin Sydserff, vol. 2, (Ross-shire, Scotland; London: Proclamation Trust Media; Christian Focus Publications, 2009), 117.

Session Eight

1. Strong's G3628, Blue Letter Bible, accessed September 16, 2021, https://www.blueletterbible.org/lexicon/g3628/kjv/tr/0-1/.

Session Nine

1. Romans 15:5,6,7,13, BibleHub, Greek Lexicon, accessed September 16, 2021, https://biblehub.com/romans/15-13.htm.

2. Robert Yarbrough, *ESV Expository Commentary: Romans–Galatians* (United States: Crossway, 2020), 200.

3. Stott, 395.

Get the most from your study.

IN THIS STUDY, YOU'LL:

- Understand how the gospel saves, transforms, and sends you out on mission.
- Unpack the vastness of all you've been given by God in salvation through Christ and the empowerment of God's Spirit at work in you.
- Learn how real rest is found in God's presence.

STUDYING ON YOUR OWN?

Watch Courtney's teaching sessions as you study, available via redemption code printed in your Bible study book.

LEADING A GROUP?

Each group member will need an *In View of God's Mercies* Bible study book, which includes video access. Because all participants will have access to the video content, you can choose to watch the videos outside of your group meeting if desired. Or, if you're watching together and someone misses a group meeting, they'll have the flexibility to catch up! A DVD set is also available to purchase separately if desired.

Browse study formats, a free session sample, video clips, church promotional materials, and more at

lifeway.com/mercies